Find Your
Family History:

Steps to get started

By Stephen M Szabados

Cover Photo: Wedding picture of my grandparents - 1923

Other Books by Author:
Finding Grandma's European Ancestors - 2012

DEDICATION

To my son Robert, my daughter Jennifer and
my wonderful grandsons Xander and Leo

CONTENTS

ACKNOWLEDGMENTS

I need to thank Michael Mulholland for the opportunity to teach Beginning Genealogy classes at Arlington Height Memorial Library. This experience helped prove the adage that the best way to learn something is to teach it. This book is based on my notes and outline from these classes.

I am grateful to Anthony Kierna at the Schaumburg Township District Library, Joan Huff at the Arlington Height Memorial Library and Frank Kaisor at the Arlington Height Memorial Library for their review and fantastic comments of the contents of this book. Jennifer Holik was especially helpful with her comments on social media.

I would also like to thank the many people that have been very patient and very tolerant with my many questions. These include many fellow researchers and also friends, relatives and especially my wife Susan who had to put-up with my many genealogy stories.

Introduction

I had wanted to know more about my family history for many years. I remembered that when I was in grade school I asked my Polish grandmother and my Hungarian grandfather questions about their birthplaces and their parents and grandparents. Unfortunately, I lost my notes and my parents and grandparents had passed by the time I decided to renew my research. This made my initial work much harder. The fact that I lost my most important sources of information before I re-started my family research shows the importance of my comments in chapter four about interviewing your older relatives.

After I re-started my research, I quickly became addicted to genealogy when I found the 1910 U.S. census and the passenger manifests for my great-grandparents. This gave me a snapshot of my family that I had not seen before. I continued to feel a thrill of excitement every time I found more documents. When I found the birth record for my Polish great-grandfather in Poland, I had difficulty breathing because of my excitement. Eventually, I was able to trace my ancestors back to the 1730s in Poland and the 1830s in Hungary.

My goals were to learn more about my family's heritage and to preserve what I found for my children and grandchildren. It has become a lifelong journey. I am thrilled when I am able to fill in more generations of my family tree. Just like reading a great novel, it is hard for me to put down my genealogy research.

Today, my passion for family history research includes helping other people find their ancestors.

My goal for this book is to outline the steps that I should have followed to begin my genealogical research. These are the steps that I now follow but they were learned after some wasted efforts and I know they will prove helpful to you. Following these steps should help you to be more efficient in your beginning research than I was.

We will cover the initial portion of genealogical research so that you will become familiar with genealogical sources. The book will give you a method to get started in your research and hopefully give you a method to find your family history. We will discuss the use of documents such as census records, passenger manifests; vital records and others that will help identify your family members and also give you information about your family's history.

However, this is not meant to be a complete overview of all aspects of genealogy. This book will only cover the use of many U.S. records. Chapter Twelve will give you suggestions on continuing education beyond the materials in this book.

I would also like to suggest reading my book "Finding Grandma's European Ancestors" when you are ready to start looking for your ancestors in European records.

Now turn to Chapter One and start your journey to your family's history.

.

1 GENEALOGY BEGINS AT HOME

Your first steps in your genealogical research begin with the documents you find at home. You need to find all the pictures and documents that you can. Collect the following if possible:

- Birth, baptism, marriage and death certificates
- Obituaries and funeral cards
- Family bibles
- Family pictures, baby books, birth announcements, wedding books, birthday books, diaries
- Passports, naturalization and immigration papers
- Land and mortgage papers
- Military papers
- Retirement papers, probate papers
- Family letters, postcards, business papers, medical records, insurance papers, newspaper clippings, and other papers

Old documents and pictures
Search the desk drawers, file cabinets and shoe boxes for "old papers" to see if your ancestors saved documents. This is especially important if they were immigrants. If they are still alive, you need to ask their permission to do this.

Baptismal or birth certificates from the old country, naturalization documents or military papers would yield extremely valuable information if found. Old letters and post cards from relatives or friends will also prove useful. The letters may be from friends or relatives that still lived where your ancestor was born. These documents may also contain references to where your ancestor left or the names of other family members. Pictures are also very important because they may show other people who may be friends or relatives. Identify all other possible relatives and track down their descendants to see if they have any treasures that pertain to your ancestors.

Other important personal documents you may find are
- Family bibles that may have lists of the births, marriages and deaths of various family members.
- Diaries that can give insight into the thoughts and interests of family members
- Newspaper clippings of births, marriages, deaths and news stories pertaining to family members.

Be prepared to find some documents that are not written in English. Some may be in the ethnic language of where your ancestors were born or they may be church documents that were written in Latin. Genealogists have compiled word lists of genealogical terms that list the term in English and in many other languages. There are many books that include examples of these lists but the most convenient source is online at Familysearch.org. Use their Wiki section and search for "word list" or "XXXX word list" where XXXX is the name of the language you need.

More documents, pictures and letters
To find personal documents such as baptismal certificates, passports, letters and postcards, search the papers of your parents and grandparents. If any were saved they will be treasures because they usually

list the birthplaces of the immigrant ancestors. Treasures may have also been saved by other relatives. Your ancestors may have lived with one of their children before they died. If they remained in the home until they died, one or two of the children may have watched over them. Track the descendants of these caretakers who may have sorted through all of the papers and pictures in the home and saved some of them. If you find documents with other relatives, ask for copies of the documents and offer to share the results of your research. Also be very careful with the originals since they may be very fragile due to age. Use copies or electronic scans in your research and store the originals in a safe place.

Remember at this point in your research, you are dealing with documents that you find in the personal papers of your parents, grandparents and other relatives. After you get the information that is in these documents organized and recorded, you can start your search for information from other sources. Interviewing older relatives and family friends Also remember to work on the easiest to find documentation, dates, and places first.

Remember that the old papers of your parents or grandparents may contain their birth certificate because they needed to show proof of their age to the Social Security Administration when they applied for for their Social Security number in order to work after 1935.

The first illustration is the Nebraska birth certificate for Harold Howard. Note that Harold's birth certificate lists the names, birthplaces and occupations of his parents.

Birth Certificate for Harold Howard

Photographs

Photos are a record of the lives of your ancestors. Photos capture the events in your ancestor lives and their lifestyles. Identifying the people in the photos is an important part of your genealogy research. This will give you another source to track down and get more documents and information. It is important that you preserve the original photos. Make copies and only take copies to family gatherings. Scanning the originals will also allow you to share copies with your family.

The next illustrations show two pictures that were in my mother's scrapbook. One is the portrait taken for my grandparent's wedding. Identifying and finding the flower girl led to more pictures and more information about my grandparents. The other picture includes two unknown women that may be relatives of my grandmother. Once identified these two women may add more information to the family history.

Wedding picture Steve and Anna Zuchowski

Picture of Anna Zuchowski with daughter, grand-daughter and two unidentified women

Cemeteries

Another important place to look when you start your genealogy research is the cemeteries where your family members were buried. The picture to the right shows a number of family members were buried in the plots surrounding this burial marker. Listed are my wife's grandmother, her two husbands and three of her children. The three children died young and were not known to my wife's generation.

This example makes finding the names of family members easy because they are all listed on the grave marker. However, many families did not use this type of marker. Once you find the grave site for your ancestor, search nearby grave markers for possible other family members. Record the inscriptions of nearby markers that have the same surname of family members. Also record the inscriptions of grave markers that have other surnames that you may have heard in the past at family gatherings. Research this list of names later to see if any can be linked to your family. Another source of cemetery records is cemetery books that were compiled by local historical or genealogical societies.

Other steps to be do as soon as possible

The next three chapters cover early steps in your family history research that should be completed as soon as possible.

- Filling out genealogy charts will help give you a picture of your family tree and help you keep relationships straight as you talk to your family members.
- Organizing your documents, pictures and notes will help you understand your next areas to research and also help you share your research with your relatives in a readable format.
- It is important to interview older your oldest relatives as soon as possible because you can not afford to loose them before you have recorded their memories and stories. However, organizing and preparing a pedigree chart before you talk to your older relatives may help them remember some important facts. A solution may be to call to schedule a visit to your relative and then try to get your material organized as much as possible before the visit.

These steps are continuous and your notes and charts should be updated as documents are reviewed and relatives interviewed. Interviews should be scheduled as soon as relatives and friends are found.

Summary for personal papers

A. Search desk drawers, file cabinets and shoe boxes for birth records, baptismal certificates, exit visas and pictures.
B. Begin filling out Genealogy Charts (see Chapter 2)
C. Organize your research to help your research and to share your research with your relatives (see Chapter 3)
D. Track down descendants of caretakers of ancestors before they died.
E. Interview the oldest members of your family as soon as possible (see Chapter 4)

2 GENEALOGY FORMS & LINEAGE SOFTWARE

The use of standard genealogical forms will help record the information you know about family members. The two forms that are used the most are the pedigree chart and the family group sheet. The next two illustrations are samples of each form. They can be downloaded from many genealogy websites such as Familysearch.org and Ancestry.com (refer the exact website addresses in the list of useful websites in the back of this book).

Pedigree Chart

Pedigree charts are the roadmaps to your family history. They may have space for four or five generations (parents, grandparents, and great-grandparents) and are sometimes called "Ancestor" or "Lineage" Charts. Spaces are usually provided for full names, dates and places of birth, marriage dates, and dates of death. Begin filling out your pedigree chart as soon as you can and take it with you to all family gatherings so the relatives can help fill in some of the blanks. Filling in your pedigree chart will help you focus your research and keep all of the relationships straight. To continue your ancestral lines beyond the first chart, start another chart using an ancestor from the last generation shown on your full chart as the first person shown on the next chart. Each person listed in the last generation shown will be the first person shown on the next chart.

Family Group Sheets

Family group sheets are the genealogy forms that are the traditional method of recording the information for each set of parents and children. This form usually shows names, dates and places of births, marriages, and deaths (see the example on page 7). You may need additional pages for large families. If one of the parents was married more than once, make another family group sheet for each additional marriage, especially if the marriage produced children. It is also very important that you cite your sources for any information that you list on this form. A family group sheet should be created for each couple on your pedigree chart.

Each piece of information concerning an ancestor and his/her family is placed on the family group sheet. Since the end result of your research efforts will be to compile complete, correct and connected families, the use of pedigree charts and family group sheets from the beginning will make the compilation much easier.

Family group sheets will help you gather, correlate, and analyze information. By carefully documenting your sources for the information listed on the family group sheet, you should be able to find clues to help you find more sources.

The samples of the Pedigree Chart and the Family Group Sheet that are shown on the next two pages can be downloaded from the Family History Forms page for the Mid-Continent Public Library at:

www.mymcpl.org/genealogy/family-history-forms

ANCESTOR CHART

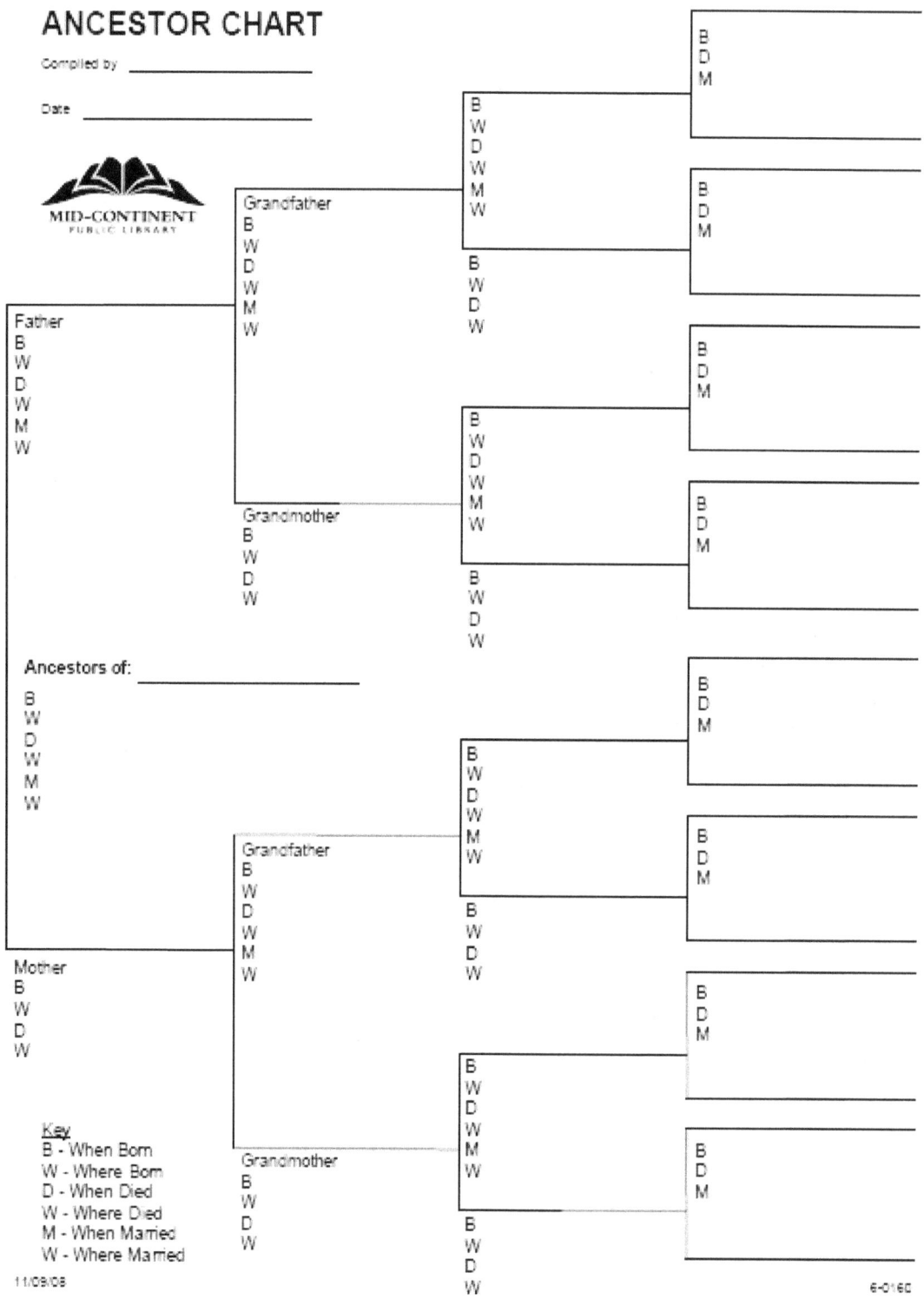

Compiled by _____

Date _____

MID-CONTINENT
PUBLIC LIBRARY

Grandfather
B
W
D
W
M
W

Father
B
W
D
W
M
W

Grandmother
B
W
D
W

Ancestors of: _____
B
W
D
W
M
W

Grandfather
B
W
D
W
M
W

Mother
B
W
D
W

Grandmother
B
W
D
W

B
W
D
W
M
W

B
W
D
W

B
W
D
W
M
W

B
W
D
W

B
W
D
W
M
W

B
W
D
W

B
W
D
W
M
W

B
W
D
W

B
D
M

B
D
M

B
D
M

B
D
M

B
D
M

B
D
M

B
D
M

B
D
M

Key
B - When Born
W - Where Born
D - When Died
W - Where Died
M - When Married
W - Where Married

11/09/08

6-0160

6

FAMILY UNIT CHART

Compiled by _____

Date _____

	DATE (day-mo-yr)	LOCATION (city / township, county, state)
HUSBAND		
Birth		
Marriage		
Death		
Burial		
His father's full name		
His mother's maiden name		
Other wives' names		
WIFE		
Birth		
Death		
Burial		
Her father's full name		
Her mother's maiden name		
Other husbands' names		

CHILDREN		DATE (day-mo-yr)	LOCATION (city / township, county, state)
#1	B		
	M		
	D		
	Spouse		
#2	B		
	M		
	D		
	Spouse		
#3	B		
	M		
	D		
	Spouse		
#4	B		
	M		
	D		
	Spouse		
#5	B		
	M		
	D		
	Spouse		
#6	B		
	M		
	D		
	Spouse		

10/08/07

7

Computer Programs for Generating Forms

There are a number of family history computer programs that are available today to help organized your genealogy information. These types of programs are also called lineage software.

Family history programs are another great tool to help organize your genealogy information. Lineage software includes the pedigree chart and family group sheets discussed above. Information added to the people listed on your lineage software will automatically update these charts and will allow you to quickly print revised pedigree charts and family group sheets. They will also provide a quick method to check relationships. Some programs have upgraded features that help the organization of your genealogical documents by allowing you to attach digital copies of your documents to the individuals in your family tree. There are a number of programs that are available on the internet with a free download. The free programs usually offer only basic functions and some are very functional and user friendly. Software programs that offer upgraded features can be purchased in retail stores or online. The upgrade features of retail programs will help make your research more efficient.

Here is a summary of some of the popular family history programs.

Free programs:

PAF (Personal Ancestral File)
Personal Ancestral File (PAF) is a genealogy management software product provided free of charge at FamilySearch.org. PAF allows users to enter names, dates, source citations, image files and other source information into a database. That information can then be used to print forms and charts, such as family group records, pedigree charts, descendant charts, and so on. PAF also allows you to share your genealogical files with other researchers using GEDCOM formatted files. It also links image files and media files to individual records. Downloads are available from FamilySearch Downloads at

https://www.familysearch.org/learn/wiki/en/FamilySearch_Downloads

PAF (Personal Ancestral File)

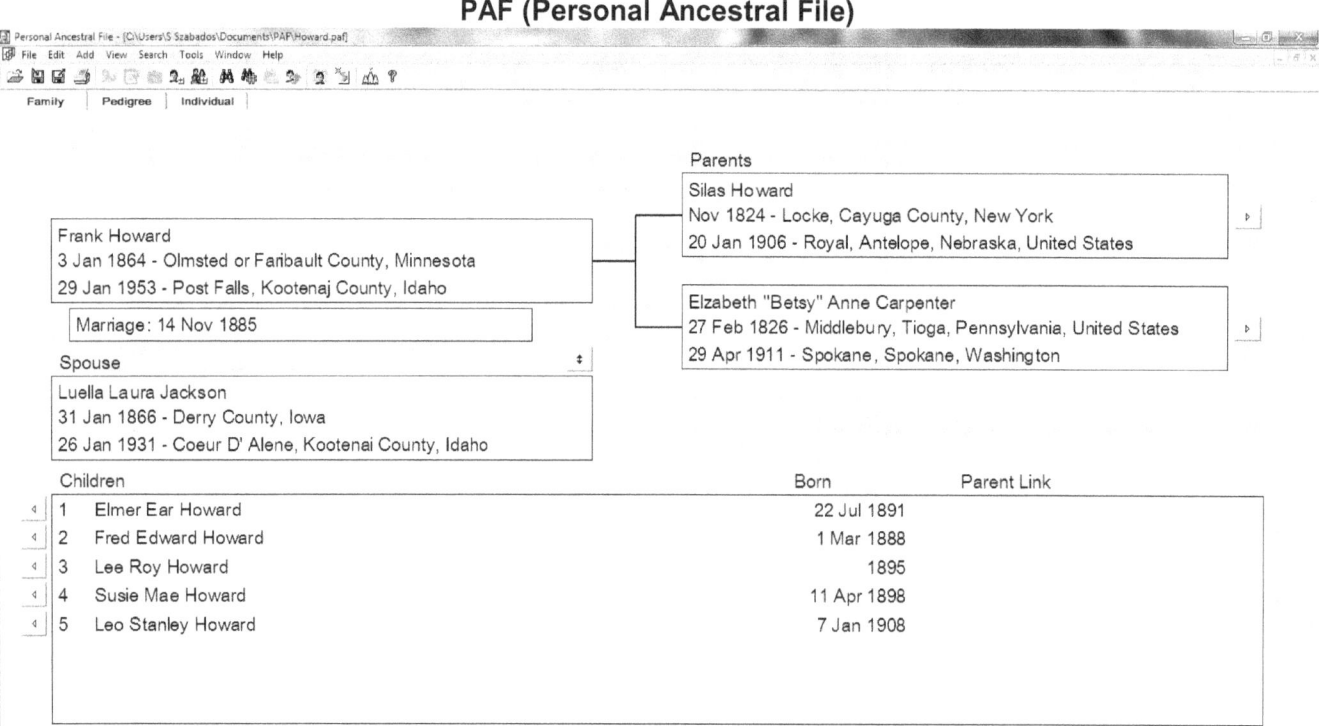

Family Tree Builder from MyHeritage.com allows basic listing of family information and printing of genealogy charts. The software automatically searches for relevant historical records amongst billions of birth, marriage, death and census records, plus newspapers and yearbooks that are available on World Vital Records. It also searches the family trees that have been uploaded by its registered members at MyHeritage.com. It offers a Windows version only.

Family Tree Builder

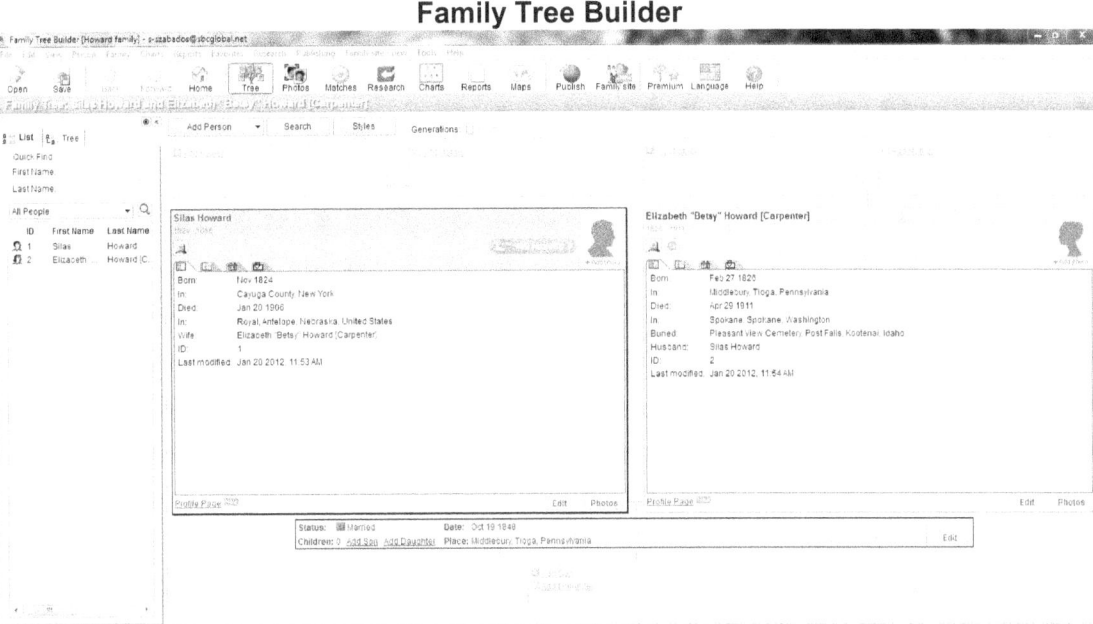

Free programs with retail versions available:

RootsMagic Essentials is a free genealogy program that contains many core features from the award-winning RootsMagic 5 retail program. It includes the basic features of the PAF and FamilyTreeBuilder programs and the added feature that allows the attaching of documents to individuals. The ability to attach photos and jpeg scans of documents adds some of the efficiencies of the retail programs. The RootsMagic retail version adds more features such as the ability to save charts as pdf files and rtf files, attach pdf files, and the ability to create a family history website. It offers a Windows version only.

RootsMagic Essentials

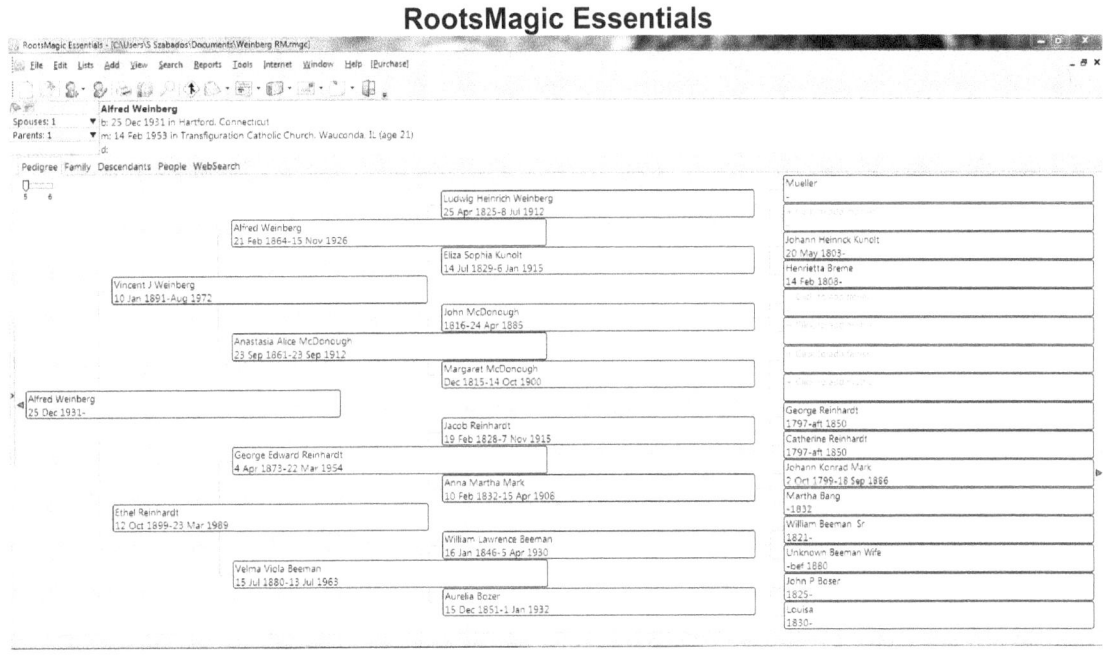

Legacy offers both a free version of its popular family history software Legacy 7.5 and a retail version. Its free version allows you to attach documents to individuals and it also has many advanced features that are in retail versions of other software programs.

Legacy 7.5 Deluxe is the retail version and it has many added features than the free version. Some of the added features in the retail version are:

- 34 more reports,
- Mapping,
- Wall Charts,
- Calendar creator,
- SourceWriter,
- Interview Reports,
- Guided Setup Wizard,
- New Powerful Searching.

Legacy 7.5 and Legacy 7.5 Deluxe is offered in a Windows version only.

Legacy 7.5

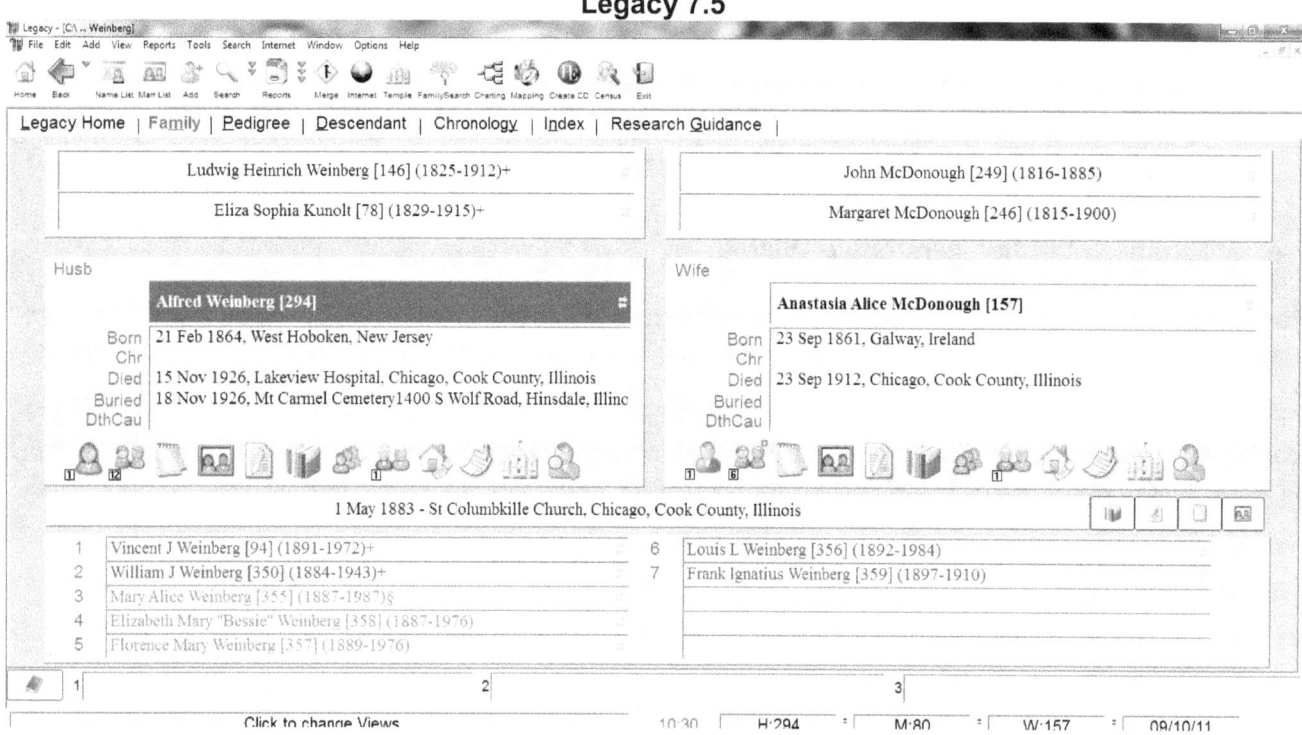

Retail only software

Reunion 9 is a genealogy software program for the Macintosh operating systems. Reunion helps you to document, store, and display information about your ancestors, descendants, cousins, etc. It records names, dates, places, facts, plenty of notes, sources of information, pictures, sounds, and videos. It shows family relationships in an elegant, graphic form -- people and families are linked in an easy-to-understand fashion. Reunion makes it easy to publish your family tree information and share it on the Web. You can also carry it on your iPod. You can automatically create common genealogy reports, charts, and forms, as well as birthday calendars, mailing lists, questionnaires, indexes, and other lists. Reunion even creates slideshows, calculates relationships, ages, life expectancies, and statistics. Reunion also creates large, graphic tree charts allowing complete on-screen editing of boxes, lines, fonts, and colors. Wall charts for family reunions are one of its specialties.

Reunion 9

FamilyTreeMaker 2012 makes it easy to discover your family history. It is available for use on Windows and Macintosh computers. It has the standard features of most of the other retail programs with these additional features.

- With a paid subscription to Ancestry.com, Family Tree Maker saves information you discover on Ancestry.com to your family tree, complete with an electronic copy of the original record. This gives you automatic access to over 5 billion U.S. records on the largest family history website.
- Write Smart Stories in two easy steps using improved page designs and templates. Each time you edit your tree, Smart Stories updates automatically.
- Store photos, audio and video files, electronic records and more data inside Family Tree Maker. Easy-to-use tools help you to manage them faster than ever before.
- Sync desktop and online Ancestry.com trees Keep your tree up-to-date wherever you are

Family Family Tree Maker 2012

The Master Genealogist is another lineage software package that is only offered in a windows version. It is a career genealogist's tool offering more built-in functions and links to online sources than other genealogy software. However, its technical language may be too much for the new researcher.

Summary for using Genealogy Forms
- A. Pedigree charts list direct ancestors
- B. Family group sheets list most facts about a family group similar to individual summaries
- C. Use lineage software to help organize your family relationships and print updated genealogy forms.
- D. Upgraded features on retail programs allow faster access to the information.

3 GET ORGANIZED AND GET STARTED

Organizing your genealogy research should go beyond developing a storage and filing system for your notes, pictures and documents. The main aspect of getting organized for a genealogist is to organize the facts that you find in your research. Your genealogy facts should be gathered, correlated, and analyzed.

To start organizing your genealogical research, I would recommend that you start compiling written summaries for each of your ancestors. I use a written summary instead of a family group sheet because the summary gives me more flexibility to include more detail in my statements of each fact. At first you may want to use both until you are more comfortable with one of them and until you begin using lineage software.

Begin organizing your research by writing a summary for the individual for whom you know the most facts. This may be you, a parent or a grandparent. In my research, I refrained from doing myself because I did not want to write an autobiography. I started with my parents. After you have recorded all the information that you have for one ancestor, you should begin recording the information for another ancestor on a new summary page.

You should find that using summaries will help you be more efficient in your research. Your summaries should include all information that you find in the documents that you have and you should continue to update your summaries with the information from the documents you find in the future. Genealogy is not just the collection of names. Your ancestors were living human beings who interacted with the people around them. Each document is a snap shot of your ancestor and each detail should be captured and analyzed. Summaries will help you gather, correlate, and analyze information.

Make sure that your statements in the summaries include where you found each fact. Be careful to keep track of the sources of your information - you will be glad you did later. The main reason to list your sources is that it will help you draw better conclusions about the accuracy of your information. Another important reason is that it may help you will find clues that help you find more sources.

The next illustrations are a sample page showing my grandfather's summary and a photo album. Note that the source of the information has been underlined in the summary. This was done only to emphasize the inclusion of the source in the summary and need not be underlined in your actual summary. Also note that the pictures have been labeled with all known information. Be sure to include unknown people in the labels for pictures because other relatives or friends may see this and be able to identify them.

Summary for Steve John Zuchowski
- Steve's name was Steve John Zuchowski on official documents but many people called him John instead of Steve. On his baptismal certificate his name is listed as Szczepan Jan Zochowski

- His baptismal certificate listed that he was born in Dmochy Kudly, Russia on December 26, 1893 to Leopold Zuchowski and Anny Dmochowski.

- He was baptized at the Catholic Parish Church, Peter and Paul the Apostles, in Czyzew.

- I have identified at least three other children of Leopold and Anny Zuchowski – Marianna (b. 1885), Boleslaw (b. 1882), and Stanislaw Zuchowski (b. 1877).

- Steve's passenger manifest listed that at age 19; he boarded the steamship SS Rhein in Bremen and departed for America on October 3, 1912. (Note that the Ancestry.com index for the manifest has Steve listed as Jan Laskowski). His occupation on the passenger manifest was listed as farmer. The SS Rhein arrived in Philadelphia on October 16, 1912. The passenger manifest listed his final destination as his brother Boleslaw Zuchowski at 1217 W Monroe St in Bloomington, Illinois.

- On his first citizenship papers in 1914, he worked as a coal miner probably for the McLean County Coal Company which was a small coal mine on the Bloomington's west side. He listed his address as 405 N Hinshaw which was close to the Monroe Street addresses of his brother and it was within walking distance of the coal mine.

- Steve's military service record stated that he enlisted in the US Army on May 11, 1917 in Chicago. Steve indicated his sister Mary Lapinska as his closest relative and her address was listed at 1324 Holt Street in Chicago. His enlistment papers were signed by Major C.E. Freeman. His service number was #745524. He served in the American Expeditionary Force in the 6th Division, 54th Regiment, Company K as a private with a rifleman's classification. His grave marker indicated that he was a member of the Illinois Mechanized Division.

- His military service records listed that he arrived in Europe on July 17, 1917. He was promoted to private 1st class on January 12, 1918 and on January 15, 1918 he was promoted to artillery mech (maybe mechanic) from CO #2 and on August 12, 1918, he was reduced to private. He participated in fighting in Varges sector from September 15, 1918 to October 12, 1918. Later, his company was assigned to troop support in Meuse Argonne offensive from November 1, 1918 to November 9, 1918. (The Meuse Argonne offensive lasted from September 26, 1918 to November 11, 1918. The 6th Division was assigned a sector near the towns of Post-A-K and Venderes).

- Sick bay records showed that Steve suffered a series of severe cases of diarrhea from November 25, 1918 to December 22, 1918 and on December 17, 1918 he was transferred from GO 111 to GHQ AEF. His military record indicated that he was not wounded. He sailed from Europe with the US Army on June 8, 1919 and arrived from Europe in the port of New York on June 10, 1919. After arrival, he and his regiment were processed on June 11, 1919 at Camp Mills on Long Island, New York for assignment or separation. He was transferred to Am K, 59th Infantry on June 16, 1919 and sent to Camp Grant near Rockford, Illinois. He was separated from the Army on June 21, 1919 at Camp Grant.

- For his service in World War I, he received the World War I Victory Medal with brass clasp for service in the Muese Argonne Defensive sector.

- The *naturalization papers for Steve's wife* indicated that he was granted citizenship in *Spartanburg, South Carolina on June 22, 1918 on Certificate 1015339.* However, the date and place on Anna's naturalization papers were in error. Steve had to be granted citizenship at the time of his honorable discharge from the US Army on June 22, 1919 at Camp Grant or in the court house in Rockford, Illinois. His military file does not note anything about his naturalization but it was a standard benefit for aliens to be granted citizenship at the time of their honorable discharge from the service. Also his 1930 census record does list that he was naturalized.

- The 1920 census indicated that Steve lived at 1408 W Mulberry Street in Bloomington and worked at the C&A railroad.

- The marriage certificate for Steve and Anna listed that they were married in St Patrick's Church in Bloomington Illinois on July 14 1923.

- The 1930 census record listed that they had two children – Regina (age 5) and John (age 3).

- Cemetery St Mary's records and stillborn death records listed that they had a third child, an infant son, who died on October 29, 1935.

- The 1924 birth certificate of their daughter Regina listed that they lived at 1316 W Market Street

- County land records listed that they purchased the house at 1418 W Mulberry on May 18, 1925 from Julia Dunn for $1100. This was where son John was born on 1/18/1927.

- County land records listed that they purchased the house at 1409 W Mulberry on November 3, 1948 for $2800 from the estate of Edmond Walthers.

- His death certificate listed that he died on Sunday, April 26, 1964

A portion of the photo album included with Steve Zuchowski's Summary - note the unknown friend in the picture on the right

Steve with family dog – abt 1940

Steve (on right) with friend (on left) at Army boot camp - 1917

After you begin recording your genealogy facts, you should decide how you want to file your summaries, charts, notes, documents and photos. Most genealogists find that a ring binder works very well and is usually convenient. Your ring binder should have a section for each ancestor that includes summaries, copies of photos, copies of documents and also brief summaries of the father's children (these are siblings of your direct ancestor).

Do not include the originals of documents and photos in your ring binder. These should be stored in a safe location using archival materials and handled infrequently. Original documents may be over one hundred years old and fragile. These documents should be placed in archival plastic sleeves to allow some viewing and will protect them from being damaged when they are handled. Try to store them in a location that will protect them from light, heat, humidity, fire and water damage. Your ring binder should include only photo copies of your documents. Place a copy of each document that pertains to an individual in the ring binder section for that individual.

Photos should be scanned and electronic copies should be distributed to your relatives in hopes that the images will survive over time. You may also consider online storage and backup options to preserve your copies. The original photo should be stored in albums with archival materials that will preserve their quality. Album type pages can be created that will include four to six images on a page and with labels below the images. Each page should include photos that pertain to one individual. These album pages could then be included in the ring binder section for that individual.

Prepare a Research Log for each ancestor
As you start accumulating papers from your genealogy research you will need to begin a research log. This is a list of sources that you have searched for a specific ancestor and is very important to successful

genealogical research. It should include notes about what you have found or did not find. It will help you for a number of reasons:

1. It will save you time by avoiding duplicate searches without a good reason
2. It will identify what has been found and not found, keep your research focused
3. It will record the source of the records that you have searched.
4. It will allow other researchers to look at your sources.

The log could be one continuous log or you could have a separate log for each person. It should be started early in your research to begin your research using proper methods.

Sample format for Research Log

Research Log

Ancestor:

Date	Place of Research	Purpose	Source	Results

Citing your sources

This section will cover the methods and reasons for citing and evaluating your sources.

As you find documents, you will need to analyze and interpret your information. This is needed because some records may contain confusing and misleading facts. It is important to state the source for all information that you find because to analyze, interpret and formulate conclusions of your data you need to know where your information came from. As a beginner to genealogy, start now to carefully note where you get every piece of information. Cite your sources and analyze your facts as you find your data.

The information you need to include for your citation is similar to the rules you used to write your term papers in high school. Citation for books should include author, title, publisher, place of publication and year of publication. Genealogy sources such as magazines, newsletters, journal articles, microfilm, documents found online and extracts should be cited with similar information. For genealogy sources you should also list the library, archive or online database where you find the information. Many of these books were printed in short runs and may be hard to find. Future researchers may wonder where you found this book and this may also be a helpful reminder to you at a later date.

For magazines, newsletters and journal articles, you should record the author, article title, periodical name, volume, issue and date of publication.

Microfilm contains published information and should be cited the same as other publication sources but add the roll number and other identifying information.

Online resources should also be cited. Elizabeth Shown Mills has published a very helpful reference to follow to capture the information from internet. It is a four page booklet - "QuickSheet Citing Online

Historical Resources." It should be available at most large genealogy libraries and can be purchased from Amazon.com.

If your information was never published such as a letter, a diary, public records, a gravestone, a church record or even an email message, you should state who wrote it, what it is, where it is now and give enough information so someone unfamiliar with your research could find that document or object again. Add notes about the condition of the item or special circumstances that impact your evaluation and analysis of it.

You may hear arguments that keeping up with sources are time consuming and too much trouble. It isn't fun but without your source information you can't evaluate what you have found. You can't analyze and draw conclusions. And you can't pass along your information because at least one family member will ask, "But how do you know?"

Evaluating your Data
Proof is the accumulation of acceptable evidence.

After finding documents, your now have to analyze and evaluate them for accuracy and relevance.

The first evaluation to make is whether the record pertains to the person or family being searched. For example, the christening record of a person with the right name about the right time may be your ancestor but if they have a common name the record may be a person with the same name and not your ancestor. Look for other details on the record that may point to your family.

Each category of records has to be evaluated differently. Some tend to be more accurate than others.
- *Original records* tend to be more accurate than derivative records. They were written close to the time of the events they record. Even a source recorded close to the time of the event may have errors because the recorder may have made a mistake.
- *Derivative records* tend to be easier to use and contain more information. However, they represent a reiteration of information from one or more other sources. The author may not have had enough information to adequately interpret the other sources. On the other hand, the compiler may have known of errors in the other sources and corrected or explained them in the compilation.
- Note that photographic copies, including microfilm, microfiche, digital, and photocopies are virtually as good as the actual document, although they may sometimes be hard to read.

The nature of the information is also a key factor when evaluating its accuracy. Information is classified as primary or secondary based on how close in time it was recorded to the event it describes.

Primary Information was recorded at or near the time of the event. The information was supplied by someone closely associated with it. Primary information is usually found in original records but not all information in an original record is "primary." For example, a death record usually contains primary information about the death, but also lists secondary information about the person's birth.

Secondary Information was recorded much later than the event or recorded by a person who was not associated with the event. The further removed the record is from the event or situation, the more secondary it is. Most derivative records and many printed records (except directories and newspapers) contain secondary information, but not all printed information is secondary. Derivative sources are, by their definition, records which have been derived - copied, abstracted, transcribed, or summarized - from previously existing sources. Original evidence usually carries more weight than derivative evidence.

If the information does not come from a primary source, it may be suspect and should be verified. Secondary information may be correct but it needs to be verified. However, the chance for error is increased with secondary information because the recorder is not familiar with the events and may have been given incorrect information in the past. The researcher needs to ask who recorded the information and how the recorder knew what happened. This will help determine if the information is primary or secondary. Sometimes you may need to use unverified information because it may be the only record available. Also it does not conflict with any proven record.

Other aspects of evaluating your information are:
- Direct statements give straightforward facts such as a death certificate will list the date of death.
- Indirect statements support a fact by inference such as a census record will list a person's age and by calculation will give you a year of birth.
- Consistent facts state information that does not conflict with other facts

Each record and each piece of evidence in a record can be evaluated individually. Proof of each fact is the accumulation of acceptable evidence. To prove a fact, you must find decisive evidence that confirms one view and excludes other reasonable possibilities. Absolute proof is seldom possible, but a sufficient degree of proof should be the goal of each researcher. You as the primary researcher are responsible for determining if the accumulated evidence provides "clear and convincing" proof of a genealogical fact.

It is reasonable to accept an original record with primary information that provides direct evidence. However, when such a source is not available, or cannot be believed because it contradicts other known facts you will need to find other sources and evaluate them for accuracy.

Summary on organizing and starting your research
A. Begin documenting your research by recording facts found in documents into summaries for each ancestor.
B. Include labeled pictures with your documents and try to identify who are in the pictures and when they were taken.
C. Record, correlate, and analyze information information in your summaries to help identify sources.
D. Keep a research log for each ancestor
E. Cite the source of your information
F. Elizabeth Shown Mills' book *Evidence Explained: Citing History Sources From Artifacts To Cyberspace* offers more details on citing your genealogical sources.

4 INTERVIEW OLDER RELATIVES AND FRIENDS

Next, begin showing your research to your older relatives and interviewing them in order to see if they have any oral history or documents to add to your research.

Saving oral history is a critical early step in your genealogical research. A great deal of family history is passed down orally through the generations. Your family's oral history may involve stories of the immigration of the family to America or it may be as simple as saving a family recipe. Remember that you are seeking information from older members of the family and their memories are at risk of being lost to time. Therefore, it should be a priority to interview your patriarchs and matriarchs of the family as soon as possible. They could be your grandparents, great-grandparents, great-uncles, great-aunts and older cousins. Even older neighbors and acquaintances of these people may have information to add. Identify the individuals in your family that seem to know the most family history and interview them as early in your research as possible.

Before your visit with relatives, prepare a list of questions and topics to cover. It is important to do this because it will help focus your conversation and their answers will help you fill in the blanks on the family tree. Obtaining the full names including nicknames and maiden names of all the relatives is very important at the start of your research. Familysearch.org has an article on their Wiki pages that lists over 1800 sample questions that can be used when interviewing older relatives. The list is available on line at:

https://wiki.familysearch.org/en/Creating_A_Personal_History.

Try to either videotape or audio record these conversations so that you have an accurate record of their comments. If using a video camera, try to have a second person control it and use a tripod to steady the filming. Taping the interview will free you up to interact with your relative and your eye contact with them may make them more comfortable so they may remember more oral history.

Also prepare for your interviews by organizing the information that you have already found. I suggest that you send your relative a note before the interview and share with them some of the questions that you may ask them. The note may help open up their memories by giving them time to remember the family stories that they heard when they were young.

You should have your researched organized in ring binders. Show your relatives your summaries and pictures. Your summaries and pictures will help establish rapport with family members and put your relatives at ease. Reviewing your research will help them recall the oral history that they have stored in their sub-conscious.

The interviews should be an equal exchange of information. The questions should flow as normal conversation and not as an interrogation. Avoid questions that seek a "Yes" or "No" answer. This gives your relatives a chance to tell their stories. Try to be a good listener:

- Don't talk or interrupt while the person is speaking.
- Don't put words in their mouths.
- Don't finish their sentences for them either.
- Let them speak until they have completed their thought before you go on to the next question.
- Include pictures in your research and ask your relatives to help identify the people in the pictures.

The two pictures shown below are two examples of pictures that I found in my mother's scrapbook that include people that I do not know and who may be distant relatives. Because my mother is in both pictures, I believe the unknown people are related to my mother and more research may uncover more relatives who immigrated. These are examples of pictures that you should show to your older relatives to try to get them to identify the people in the pictures and ask when and where the pictures were taken. This may help get them to start talking and remembering some of the oral history they have stored in their subconscious.

Picture of my grandmother (far right), my mother, me (between my grandmother and mom), my sister and unknown family taken near Bloomington about 1952 (based on my estimated age)

Picture of my mother sitting near WW I monument in Smith Park in Chicago (Grand and Western Avenues.) The two women may be relatives. Picture circa 1945

Don't try to complete the Interview in one sitting. You should keep your interviews to no more than a couple of hours unless the person feels otherwise. People get tired after talking for a while. You should plan on more than one session. This gives you a chance to follow-up on various aspects of the oral history that you capture and also gives your relative time to remember more aspects of the family history.

The interview may also reveal that other members of the family are doing genealogy research and this could lead to exchanging more information and copies of documents.

Also remember that memories often fade and facts get confused with other facts. However, the information you obtain through oral interviews may exist nowhere else and must be taken at face value. Of particular value is information associated with pictures, documents, and other records. Also of interest are the stories, anecdotes and family traditions. Treat the oral history that you hear as treasures. However, if some of the facts do not seem accurate, remember that some parts of the story may have a grain of truth so include all of the stories and add your comments and concerns. Future generations may be able to find more facts that sort out your concerns and resolve the problem areas of the stories.

After the interview, transcribe your conversations if you used recording equipment. If you did not record the conversation, review and summarize your notes while the conversation is still fresh in your mind. Make lists of future questions and lists of future research that are needed.

Summary of interviewing

1. Interviewing older relatives is a critical early step in genealogical research
2. Interview relatives as soon as possible. Don't wait until tomorrow because your relative may not be available.
3. Prepare a ring binder with your summaries, charts and photos to show your progress to your relative
4. Interviews should be an equal exchange of information and should not be an interrogation.
5. Establish rapport with family members prior to interviewing them
6. Avoid questions that seek a "Yes" or "No" answer
7. Let your relative talk (this may help them feel more comfortable
8. Record interviews if possible (ask permission)
9. Try to check the information from oral histories – treat information as clues
10. Re-visit your relative after you have new and interesting information to show them. This may turn on the memory for another story for them to tell you.

5 CENSUS - START SEARCHING

Beyond personal papers and oral family history

After you have found all the shoe box documents and you have interviewed many of the living relatives, you have to begin searching for records. Most of the records that you will find will add to your family history and help point the way to more information. However, before you start searching for more records, please remember that some of the information that you have and will find may be confusing, misleading and wrong. To overcome these confusing records, you have to remember you need to always analyze your information and interpret what you find. Does the information make sense and is there corroborating information in other documents. Evaluating data as you find the documents will help keep you on the right track of finding your ancestors. If you use erroneous data you will waste time researching people that are not in your family.

Another facet to remember is that some information that you find may be embarrassing but you can not change it. You have to accept what you find and continue your search one generation at a time. You can read more about evaluating your information please read the next chapter . Now let's cover some of the sources and types of records.

Using the Internet

Using online resources is a very good strategy to use at the start your search for documents and information outside of your home. Records in most online databases can be searched by the names of your ancestors. This will allow you to find more documents in a shorter time period and this will maximize your initial research efforts. Note that the online resources are only a place to start your research. Some of the online databases have images of the documents and some are only indexed. If images are available they can be viewed and downloaded. If the databases only offer a summary of information that was extracted from documents you will need to look at the description for the databases which will give you clues on the location of the actual documents. It is important to obtain the actual document because the online index may show inaccurate information. The actual document will probably show the accurate information and the document will probably list more information than what was listed in the index.

The number of genealogical databases on the internet has increased dramatically in recent years. It is difficult to name all of the online resources that are available but Ancestry.com and Familysearch.org are the two major genealogy websites. You should be able to find a great deal of information from the databases on these two websites. (Note that the Ancestry.com databases are available at many libraries on Ancestry Library Edition. Please remember that if I refer to Ancestry.com, you should understand that Ancestry Library Edition is also included.) Many U.S. states and counties have also made many of their records available online and these sources should also be aggressively used in your initial research.

Here are samples of the most useful records that you can find online either as an index or as the document.

- Census – state and federal (most can be found in online databases)
- Birth (indexes and some documents are available in online databases)
- Marriage (indexes and some documents are available in online databases)
- Death (indexes and some documents are available in online databases)
- Obituaries (many are available in online databases)
- Passenger manifests (most can be found in online databases)
- Naturalization papers (many index cards can be viewed online but most actual documents must be ordered from the National Archives or county courts)

The pages in this and the next chapters will give an explanation of the genealogical importance of each of these records and discuss some of the sources where they can be found.

Census Records

The U.S. Federal Census was mandated in 1787 by the US Constitution to count the U.S population to determine representation in the U.S. House of Representatives. Today it is also used by the states to determine the representation in their state Houses of Representatives. The U.S. Constitution requires that the census should be done in 1790 and every ten years thereafter.

Census records are a list of individuals and families and are constantly used by genealogists to identify ancestors. The researcher must find those records that connect each generation to parents in previous generations. One mis-step in making these links may send you off on someone else's family tree. Generally start with the 1940 census or the latest before your ancestor's death and work backward in time to indentify each set of parents.

States and territories also conducted censuses. Some were merely head counts but some had very useful genealogical information. Most of the state and territorial census records can be found in databases at Ancestry.com and Familysearch.org.

The format of the census records for 1790 through 1840 required listing only basic information that was needed to give the Federal government an accurate head count. These early census records included the names of only the head of the household, state, county, town, counts of the household by age ranges and gender, and the number of slaves by gender.

Info from 1790-1840 census records:
(Designed to count population)
- State of residence – all
- County of residence - all
- Township of residence – 1800 and after
- Name of head of Household – all
- Number of people in house hold - 1790
- Number in household by gender & age range – 1800 and after
- Number of slaves- all
- Number of free non-whites in household -all
- Deaf, dumb, blind, or insane – 1840
- Education and able to read & write – 1840
- Type of industry house hold members worked in – 1840
- Names of Revolutionary War pensioners - 1840

The U.S. Federal Census records from 1850 and after are more than a list of names. They contain a significant amount of data that can add rich facts to your family history. The information found beyond the column of names on these documents add information about where your ancestors lived, when they were married, where they were born, where their parents were born and much more. Use all of the information on census records to maximize your research results and use both Federal and State census records.

The census records in 1850 and thereafter included the names of all household members and many more demographic questions. Below is a summary of the Information available from the 1850 through 1930 census records.

- State of residence – all
- County of residence - all
- Township of residence – all
- Name of head of Household – all
- Names of Household members – all
- Relationship to head of household – 1880 and after
- Number of children of mother and how many were alive – 1900 and 1910
- Marriage – 1850 (if within one year), 1890 (if married within the census year), 1900 and 1910 (gives number of years married), 1930 (gives age when first married)
- Race – 1850 and after
- Address – 1880 and after
- Age and birthplace – state or country - all
- Where parents were born – 1880 thru 1930
- Year of arrival – 1900, 1910 and 1930
- Naturalization – 1890 and after
- Occupation – all
- Employment - 1930 & 1940
- Value of real estate – 1850, 1860, 1870, 1930, 1940
- Value of personal property - 1860, 1870
- Home ownership – 1900 and after
- Residence in 1935 - 1940
- Education or ability to read and write – 1900 and after
- Highest level of education - 1940
- Deaf, dumb, blind, or insane – 1850-1890 and 1910
- Union or Confederate survivor -1910
- Military veteran - 1930
- Mother tongue – 1920 & 1930
- Households with radios - 1930

In April 2012, the 1940 census was released and thirty-four questions were asked of all individuals. It is also interesting that sixteen of the questions asked to all individuals were questions about employment. This was dramatic increase over previous years and was probably done to measure how the United States was recovering from the depression of the 1930s. An additional sixteen questions were asked of only the individuals listed on lines 19 and 29 on each census page.

Unfortunately most of 1890 census was destroyed in a 1921 fire. Ancestry.com has developed databases such as state census records, city directories and voter registration lists that cover years before and after 1890 that may cover some of the information lost when the 1890 federal census was lost in the fire.

Federal census records can be found on a number of online databases - Ancestry.com, Familysearch.org and HeritageQuest. The Ancestry.com and Familysearch.org have indexed all individuals listed on the census records to allow searches by name. However, HeritageQuest has only indexed the head of household.

For the genealogical researcher deciphering the census records for 1790 through 1840 presents more of a challenge because these records only give the names of the head of household. When I need to decipher these records, I use the following method:

1. Use personal information & family trees and other information posted by other researchers <u>as clues</u>
   a. Develop a list of names and birthdates of children
   b. Look for embedded narratives in online family trees
   c. Look to see if the researchers listed their sources
   d. Also search and post queries on Genforum.com and Rootsweb.com if needed
2. Use non-census documents to help identify more facts
   a. Vital records (birth, marriage and death)
   b. Cemetery records (county websites)
   c. Military (Colonial militia and Revolutionary War pension)
3. Search for published family history books and family genealogy websites.
4. Search for narratives on specific individuals or anyone with the family surname (keep within a general geographic area).
5. Familiarize yourself with the history of the area with focus on the dates for statehood, the formation of counties and the approximate time your family moved to the locale plus when they left.
6. Collect census records of all possible family members (same surname) in same county for all years possible.
7. Analyze and Compare census information
   a) Compare list of known family members to listed household members by gender and age group on census records found.
   b) Try to match known children to family members listed in households of early census records.
   c) Eliminate records that are missing family members that should be on record (small children are best to try to match because teenagers may be living and working in another household.
   d) Use non-census records to try to fill-in the names of the remaining unknown household members (be sure to consider dates of deaths of parents and include aged parents in some households).
   e) Compare results to online trees.
   f) Try to confirm results with two different documents – if not keep searching for verification.

Analyze & Compare Info for Washington Wilmot's Family 1820 to 1850 census records

	Birth Year	Census Range	1820 Census	1830 Census	1840 Census	1850 census
Washington	1783	1781-1790	1	1	1	1
Mary	1792	1791-1800	1	1	1	1
Jemina Hurley	1764	1761-1770			1	died 1844
George	1807	1801-1810	1	1	Married	Married
Mary	1810	1801-1810		1	Married	died 1840's
Priscilla	1811	1811-1815	1	1	Married	Married
Permilla	1814	1811-1815	1	1	Married	Married
Isaac	1818	1816-1820	1	1	w/George	Married
Unknown Boy #1	1816-20	1816-1820	1	1	Not found	Not found
Willard	1820	1816-1820	1	1	w/George	Married
Nathan	1823	1821-1825		1	1	Married
Elizabeth	1823	1821-1825		1	1	1
Sarah	1825	1821-1825		1	1	1
Abigail	1827	1826-1830		1	1	1
Andrew	1829	1826-1830		1	1	1
Morris F	1831	1831-1835			1	1
Jemina	1835	1831-1835			1	1
Unknown boy #2	1836-40	1836-1840			1	Not Found
Total # children in Household			6	12	7	6

Mortality Schedules

Mortality schedules were compiled at the same time as the 1850 through 1880 census schedules. These were schedules of everyone who had died in the previous year from June 1 of the year prior to the census to May 31 of the census year. They listed the name, age, sex, marital status, race, occupation, birthplace, cause of death and length of illness of the people who passed away during the past year. This could be used as a source for death information because it should represent about ten percent of the deaths that occurred between each census and they were recorded before most states required the recording of deaths. Granted that these schedules will not list all deaths but they will give you a chance to find a record of death that does not exist in any other place. If you find your ancestors in these schedules, you will add a tremendous amount of information to your family history.

Slave Schedules

Slaves were counted on the census records from 1790 to 1840 and the counts distinguished the sexes but the ages were not segregated.

The 1850 and 1860 census added separated pages for counting the slaves. These schedules listed the slaves by their owner and listed their age, sex and race (black or mulatto). The enumerators were instructed to name the slaves who were 100 years old or older but this rarely occurred.

Indian Census Rolls

If you have Native American ancestors you may find your ancestors in the Indian Census Rolls that were taken from 1885 through 1940. These records were used by the government to allocate resources and funds to the various reservations and the records listed the individual's Indian name, their English name, their age, gender and relationship to the head of household. Many of these records are available on Ancestry.com.

Where to find copies of the Census records:

U.S. Federal Census records are best searched using online databases which can be found at Ancestry.com, HeritageQuest and Famlysearch.org. The census records for various states can be found at Ancestry.com and Familysearch.org. Try both websites because some of the state census records are available on only one but not the other of these to websites. I normally search the U.S. Federal census records at Ancestry.com first because the have the largest collect of records and their search engine seems to be easier to use. Familysearch.org also has a large collection but some years will have the information indexed but the images are not available. The Federal census databases at HeritageQuest can be accessed at most libraries but not all years are available and they have only indexed the heads of household for each family. Also the search engine that HeritageQuest uses does not recognize possible spelling variations or allow wildcard characters.

Summary for Census Records

1. Use census records to identify the parents of your ancestors to add generations to your family tree.
2. Also use State census records when available
3. Be sure to extract all of the information listed on census records. This information about your ancestors can add to your family history.
4. Use non-census documents to help decipher the census records for 1790 through 1840.
5. Using online databases to search census records for your ancestors is more efficient because this will allow you to search by their names.

6 VITAL RECORDS - START SEARCHING

This chapter will discuss birth, marriage and death records

Birth Records

Birth records are important sources of family history information. If found, these records are civil birth registers, birth certificates and church baptismal registers. Most birth records list the name of the parents which normally includes the maiden name of the mother. The maiden name of the mother is critical to finding the mother's parents and extending her branch of your family tree. Some records also include the home address for the family and the occupation of the father.

After finding the birth record you will be able to:
- Search for the mother's parents.
- Take pictures of where your ancestor was born.
- Look for newspaper birth announcements that may contain more information.

The record that you find may be the original that was filed at the time of the event. It may be an amended record that was revised to reflect corrections or new information such as the addition of the given name for the child. It may also be a delayed birth record that was created to establish a legal birth record for an individual who was born before the registration of births was required.

Birth records that were created in the 1900s are usually easy to find but I have found it difficult to find records for individuals born prior to 1900. This may be true because marriages and deaths were recorded by churches and civil offices before birth records were required. Most early birth records were recorded by the church the parents attended but many were also lost when small churches disbanded as the population moved west and the records were not given to neighboring churches or to local governments.

Delayed birth records were issued to establish a legal birth record for an individual who was born before it was mandatory for a birth certificate to be issued or for some other reason where one was not filed at birth. A delayed birth record was issued because the person needed it to proof their birthdates for various reasons. The creation of Social Security in 1933 caused delayed birth records to become very important when people had to provide proof of their birthdates when applying for a social security number. To create a delayed birth record, individuals normally applied to the local courts and provided documents such as affidavits by people who were witness to the birth or by people who were close to the family at the time of the birth. Secondary documents such as newspaper birth announcements may have also been part of the documentation.

Today the genealogy researcher's best source for birth records are the Familysearch.org databases and their catalog of films. Some records are also available on Ancestry.com and Worldvitalrecords.com. Some of the databases found on these websites include the digital copy of the actual record and you will be able to download this copy. If the birth information found on these websites is indexed information, you should note the source of their information and attempt to get a copy of the actual document from the source that they list. If these online sources do not list the birth records you should try the local genealogy or historical society in the area where your ancestor lived because many have files of newspaper articles for the surnames in the area. Also the websites sponsored by US Genweb and Genealogy Trails History Group may have birth information listed that they gleaned from the birth announcements in the historic issues of the local newspaper.

The illustration below shows the index page from Ancestry.com for a Kentucky birth record. When you click on the image in the upper right hand corner, you will be able to see and download the image of the actual page from the 1854 birth register for Pulaski County, Kentucky

Birth record from Kentucky on Ancestry.com

Kentucky Birth Records, 1852-1910 about Aaron Vanhook

Name:	**Aaron Vanhook**
Birth Date:	7 Apr 1854
Birth County:	Pulaski
Ethnicity:	White
Gender:	Male
Father's Name:	Geo Vanhook
Mother's name:	Nancy Landford
County of Residence:	Pulaski

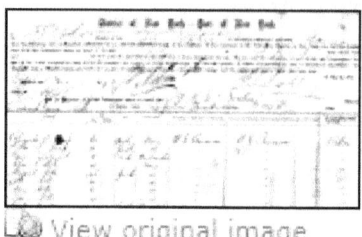

View original image

Save This Record

Attach this record to a person in your tree as a source record, or save for later evaluation.

Save ▾

Source Information:
Ancestry.com. *Kentucky Birth Records, 1852-1910* [database on-line]. Provo, UT, USA: Ancestry.com Operations Inc, 2007.
Original data: Kentucky. *Kentucky Birth, Marriage and Death Records – Microfilm (1852-1910)*. Microfilm rolls #994027-994058. Kentucky Department for Libraries and Archives, Frankfort, Kentucky.

Description:
This database contains county birth records from Kentucky for the years 1852-1910. Information available in these records includes: name of child, gender, race, birth date, birth place, parents' names, parents' birthplaces, and parents' ages. Learn more...

The next illustration is an index page from the Ancestry.com Indiana birth records. No images of the actual record are available on this database and you will have to review the citation information for this database to see where you can get a copy of the actual document. Note that the Source information section does not tell you this. When you click on learn more, the information shown will expand to information shown in the illustration on page 32. This information directs you to order a copy either from the county heath department or the Division of Vital Records.

Ancestry.com Index Page for the Indiana Births Database

Indiana Births, 1880-1920 about Sarah E Jones

Name:	**Sarah E Jones**
Father:	Morgan
Mother:	Sarah Richards
County:	Madison
Gender:	Female
Birth Date:	Apr 30
Reference:	Madison County, Indiana Index to Birth Records 1882 - 1920 Inclusive Volume I Letters A - K Inclusive Madison County, Indiana Index to Birth Records 1882 - 1920 Inclusive Volume I Letters H - K Inclusive
Book:	CH-2
Page:	55

Save This Record

Attach this record to a person in your tree as a source record, or save for later evaluation.

Save ☑

Source Information:
Ancestry.com. *Indiana Births, 1880-1920* [database on-line]. Provo, UT, USA: Ancestry.com Operations Inc, 2000.
Original data: Works Progress Administration. *Index to Birth Records*. Indiana: Indiana Works Progress Administration, 1938-1940.

Description:
This database indexes the birth records for many of the counties in the State of Indiana, USA, from 1880 to 1920. Information that may be found in this index for each entry includes name, gender, father, mother, county of birth, birth date, and source notes. Learn more...

Expanded description of the Indiana Births Index, 1880-1920

Source Information

Ancestry.com. *Indiana Births, 1880-1920* [database on-line]. Provo, UT, USA: Ancestry.com Operations Inc, 2000.
Original data: Works Progress Administration. *Index to Birth Records*. Indiana: Indiana Works Progress Administration, 1938-1940.

About Indiana Births, 1880-1920

Birth records for the state of Indiana were recorded by the county health office beginning in 1882. The WPA began to index vital records, county-by-county for the entire state, but the agency was abolished before it was completed. This database indexes births for thirty-one of the counties indexed by the WPA. Taken from copies of the original works from the WPA, these records will prove useful for those seeking ancestors in the state of Indiana.

Counties included in this database are:

Adams, Allen, Boone, Cass, Clay, Davies, De Kalb, Harrison, Hendricks, Henry, Howard, Huntington, Jay, Johnson, Knox, Madison, Martin, Monroe, Morgan, Orange, Owen, Parke, Perry, Posey, Putnam, Spencer, Vanderburgh, Vigo, Warrick, and Washington Counties, Indiana.

Birth and death records were recorded by the county health office beginning in 1882 where they remain before mandatory recording with the state board of health began in October 1907 for births and January 1900 for deaths. Certified copies may be obtained from either the county heath department or the Division of Vital Records.

Taken from *Indiana, Ancestry's Red Book* by Carol L. Maki, edited by Alice Eichholz. (Salt Lake City, UT: Ancestry Incorporated, 1992).

The next illustration shows the search result from the Familysearch.org database for *Arkansas Births and Christenings, 1880-1893*. Note that an image of the actual document is not available. However, the record lists that the image if available from the Familysearch.org catalog on film number 1293974.

Search result from Familysearch.org database for *Arkansas Births and Christenings, 1880-1893*

Arkansas Births and Christenings, 1880-1893 for Ora Jones

« Back to search results

name	Ora Jones
gender	Female
baptism-christening date	
baptism-christening place	
birth date	20 Jan 1892
birthplace	Jonesboro, Craighead, Arkansas
death date	
name note	
race	White
father's name	Richard Jones
father's birthplace	Arkansas
father's age	
mother's name	Mary Ann Benson
mother's birthplace	Arkansas
mother's age	
indexing project (batch) number	C73550-4
system origin	Arkansas-EASy
source film number	1293974
reference number	Item 1 p 148

No image available

Q Search collection

i About this collection

Film Number

You may find that it will be difficult to find birth records for your ancestors who were born in colonial times up to the early nineteenth century. Civil records may be available but church records would be the best source to search for birth records from this time period, especially in New England states.

Many of these records have been compiled and saved in state or county historical archives or museums. Census records are a good source to find clues as to where to look and narrow the year range of your search.

In some cases, family bibles may be the only source for birth information. This is especially true for the birth and death information for a child who died very young. If your immediate family did not inherit your family bible your may have to network with other relatives to find one. Many family bibles have been saved by local genealogy and historical societies. Some bible can also be found in the LDS Family History Library card catalog.

Other sources include wills, probate records; newspapers birth announcements, obituaries; cemetery records; headstones; and biographical collections.

Summary Birth Records
- Birth records will list the names of the parents and should give the maiden name for the mother.
- Some online databases have images of the actual documents but many offer only indexes of extracted information.
- If images of the actual document are not available online, you will need to obtain from the county office, the state archives or the local historical or genealogy society.

Marriage Records
Marriage records may also be a great source of information of your ancestors. Churches and governments often kept marriage records before they began documenting births and deaths. Also remember that if the ceremony was performed in a church, the event may have been recorded in both the civil registers and the church registers. Important genealogical information that may be found on marriage records are the age of the bride and groom, the names of their parents and their birthplace. Most marriage applications ask where the bride and groom were born and most church registers have a space in the record for where they were baptized. Always look in both church and civil records for the marriage record because one record may list more information about the town such as district or county. Since the bride and groom are there to give the information, the information should be accurate although spelling errors may occur. Other interesting facts that may be found on the marriage records are the names of the witnesses, the name of the official who performed the ceremony and where the bride and groom lived before the ceremony. Remember to also search for the marriage records for their siblings and cousins - especially if they were born in the "old country."

The first step to find the marriage record for your ancestor will be finding out when they were married. Use the following sources for finding when your ancestors were married:
1. If a family bible exists look there first.
2. Family oral history may give an approximate time but this may be a very vague and inaccurate date.
3. The birth year for the oldest child but this is only a clue. The parents may have married after the birth or many tears before.
4. Other important sources to find the date are the 1900, 1910 and 1930 Federal census records which list information that you can use to calculate the approximate year of the marriage. The 1900 and 1910 census records list the number of years they were married and the 1930 record lists the age when they were first married. After doing the math you will have the approximate year of the marriage. Although, this is not an exact date it will help narrow the search. Note that the 1930 census asked for their age at the time of their first marriage and if you find that the

number of years married for the spouses do not match, the spouse with the greater number of years was probably married to a prior wife.

Find when your ancestor married - 1900, 1910 & 1930 Census will give approximate year

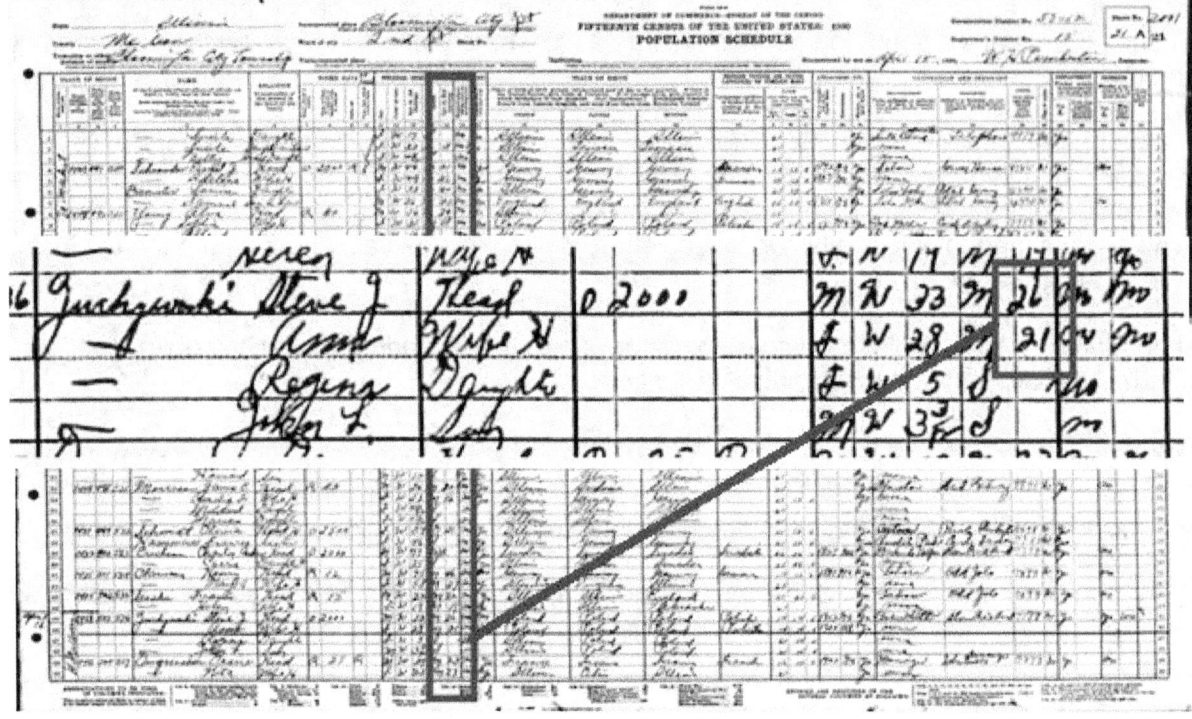

5. Online marriage indexes by state usually cover a limited time range but if your ancestor is listed you will then have both the "when" and the "where" information you need to get the actual document. The Family Search Wiki page titled "Summary of United States Marriage Records' lists the available online marriage indexes by state that are in the databases at familysearch.org and ancestry.com. I have found some indexes by googling the phrase "XXXXX marriage index'" where XXXX is the name of the state of interest. Using this method I have found marriage indexes for Illinois, for Wisconsin, for Minnesota and the Western States (this index includes Alaska, Arizona, California, Colorado, Idaho, Montana, Nevada, New Mexico, Oregon, Utah, Washington and Wyoming).

Sample of State of Illinois Marriage Index at
http://www.cyberdriveillinois.com/departments/archives/marriage.html

Illinois Statewide Marriage Index, 1763–1900

Click here for information about how to obtain copies of original marriage records.

Groom	Bride	Date	Vol./Page

5 records are displayed.
The maximum number displayed is 500. If a MORE button appears below, click for additional reco

SITTIG, AUGUST	SCHAFER, MAGGIE	1897-02-17	00K/0186 0
SITTIG, BERNHARDT	MYERS, ELLA	1891-01-10	00J/0229
SITTIG, REINHARD	GIESE, WILHELMINE	1895-03-15	00K/0103 0
SITTIG, REINHART	GIESE, WILHELMINA	1887-11-23	00J/0106
SITTIG, RICHARD	SCHAEFER, ELIZABETH	1895-12-25	00K/0138 0

6. Other important sources for marriage information are the files of the local genealogical and historical societies. Many of these groups have copied pages or extracted information from local newspapers on marriages and deaths. Their websites usually list their collections and most will provide copies of the information for a nominal fee. Find their website, check their collections and then call or write them with your request. . Search the genealogy websites by state, county and ethnic group to find these marriage indexes.

Below is a portion of the directory for the Polish Genealogical Society of America (located in Chicago) and it shows the lists of marriage indexes for the Polish churches in Chicago and nearby counties (see below). I have also found marriage information on many county genealogy websites.

PGSA Marriage Indexes

- Marriage Records - In addition to the following, look in this directory for a specific city or region.

  - **Marriage Indices for Parishes in Poland**

  - **Marriage Index to Polish Parishes in Chicago thru 1915**

  - **Genealogical Hints**

  - **Poznan Marriage Project**

    An index of marriages from the former Polish province of Poznan (Posen).

  - St. Joseph County, IN

    - **Marriage Record Database**

  - St. Paul, MN and vicinity

    - **Birth/Baptism Record Database**

    - **Marriage Record Database**

Determine where they were married

Before you request marriage records you will have to know where they were married. Of course if the marriage is found in one of the indexes, the location should also be indicated. If census records were the only indicator of when they were married, then the county listed on the census record may be where they were married if they did not move after the marriage. However, sometimes they may have been married in nearby counties instead of the county listed on the census. This difference in the county may have been due to the location of the church or that they chose to be married in a county that had easier marriage restrictions or they may have been married at a romantic location.

Where to obtain marriage records

I have found that the state of Washington have made the images of their marriage records available online. Some counties also allow for copies of these records to be ordered online. However, for other locations the marriage records normally are obtained from county offices or state archives using the mail. If you have identified the church where they were married, calling the church may find a helpful secretary who could send you a copy of the record. Also remember that church staff may have other duties and not have time to search their records for old marriage records - you may have to review the church records in person to obtain your information. Another important source for civil and church marriage records is the films from Family Search Centers. The films cover a limited time range but if the year of the marriage is not available on the films, then county and state records would be your only source.

Also remember to search for marriage records for children, siblings and other relatives who were born in the "old country" and married in America.

Below is the marriage application for my grandparents that I obtained from the McLean County Clerk's office in Bloomington Illinois. The clerk's office charged $15 for the two page copy which included the application and the certificate. Note that the name of her birthplace is misspelled but it did give me a name for a clue. Note that it also gave the names of her parents which were also a major help in tracing my grandmother's ancestors.

Marriage license application for Anna Chmielewski

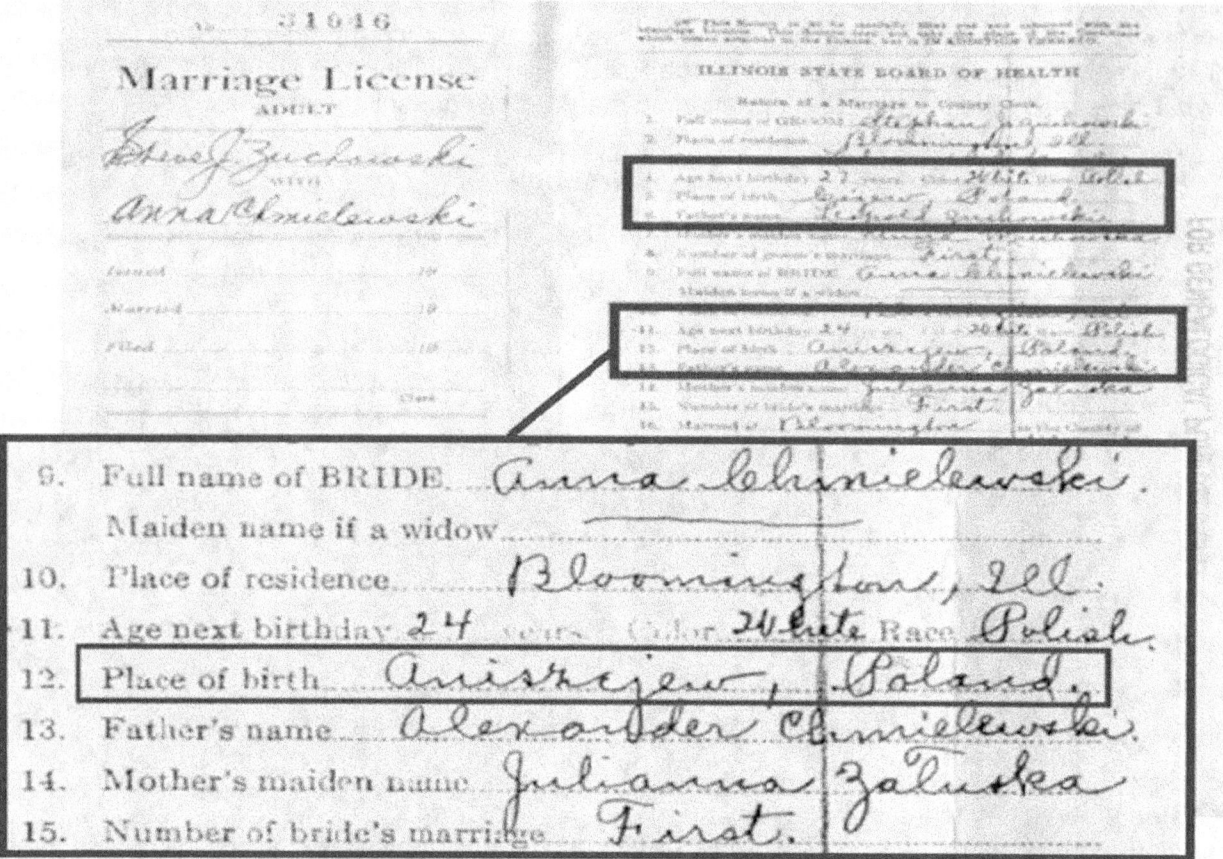

I have found that some counties saved only a copy of the marriage license and not the application. The license usually does not indicate where the bride and groom were born. In this case, check the license for the name of who performed the marriage. If the marriage was performed by a minister or priest, you will have a clue on where to look for the church record. Another indicator to find the church record is the religion and ethnic background of your ancestor. Small areas may have had only one church of a specific religion. Also in large urban areas, certain churches attracted one ethnic group because the service was performed in their native language.

The following illustration is a copy of the page from the marriage register of St Ludmila's Church in Chicago that lists the marriage of Mary Strugar who was the sister of my wife's grandmother. St Ludmilla's was attended by the Slovenian immigrants who had immigrated to Chicago. Note that this register has a column for the date and place of Baptism (Datum et Locus Baptismi). Catholic priests would normally list the parish of baptism in their marriage registers to insure that both the bride and groom were baptized so he could perform the marriage in the church. This copy was obtained from a Family History Center (FHC) film. The FHC films were created through efforts by the Church of the Latter Day Saints to help document their ancestors. I was able to rent this film at one of the Family History Centers and found this document by viewing the film. Today the images from this film are available in the databases on Familysearch.org.

Church marriage register for Mary Strugar (sister of my wife's grandmother)

NOMINA ET RESIDENTIAE	DATUM ET LOCUS BAPTISMI	PATRES NOMINA
Leben Frank	24. VIII. 1886 Selca - Gor. - Carniola	Leben Martin Mary C. Benedikt
Narobe Maria	8. IX. 1885. Domžale - Carn.	Narobr Natthisias Mary C. Basca
Grill Frank	7. XII. 1885 Bušinec - Toplice - Carn.	+ Grill John Ursula C. Bradač
Strugar Mary	21. V. 1889. Črnomelj - Carn.	Strugar Jacob Mary C. Stonič

Summary for marriage records
1. Find out when ancestors were married in U.S. – family bible, census records or online indexes
2. Find out where couple was married – family bible, census records or online indexes
3. Where to obtain documents – county clerks, state archives, Church registers, FHC films, online databases

Death Records

Death records such as death certificates and obituaries may list some important genealogy information for the researcher. I have seen the age of the deceased listed, their place of residence, place of death, name of their spouse, name of their parents and their place of birth. However this information is not listed on all the documents that I found. We should also be concerned with the accuracy of the information on these documents because it may have been provided by someone who may have not known the facts.

1. Many times the record only lists the country of birth and not the town.

2. Many times the birth place is listed as "unknown" on death certificates.

3. The information may be wrong because the information was given by someone who did not know or remember the correct information.

4. If the death certificate or obituary lists a birthplace, use it as a place name to include on your list of clues but remember that it may be the least accurate.

In order to judge the accuracy of the information on death records, review the death certificate for the name of the informant. The information may be accurate if the informant was also born in the same birth place. If the informant was one of the children who were born after immigration, the information should be used carefully and the place name given may be a phonetic spelling.

Below are some examples of death certificates that I found useful in identifying the birthplaces of ancestors.

The next illustration is the death certificate for Waleryan Puchalski. It lists the town of Glebokie, Poland as his birthplace. The informant on the certificate was his wife Mary who he met and married in Chicago,

Illinois. Since Mary was not born in the same area as Waleryan, Glebokie is probably the phonetic spelling of his birthplace. This was the only document found for Waleryan that listed a town for his birthplace. The only other clue of where he was born was that Russia was listed on the 1900 and 1910 census records. I found fifteen different locations that could be variations of the Glebokie name but only three were in areas that were part of Russia in 1910. I also used the fact that his occupation was a shoemaker to find his birth record in the village of Hlybokae in present day Belarus which had a shoemaker school.

Death certificate for Waleryan Puchalski

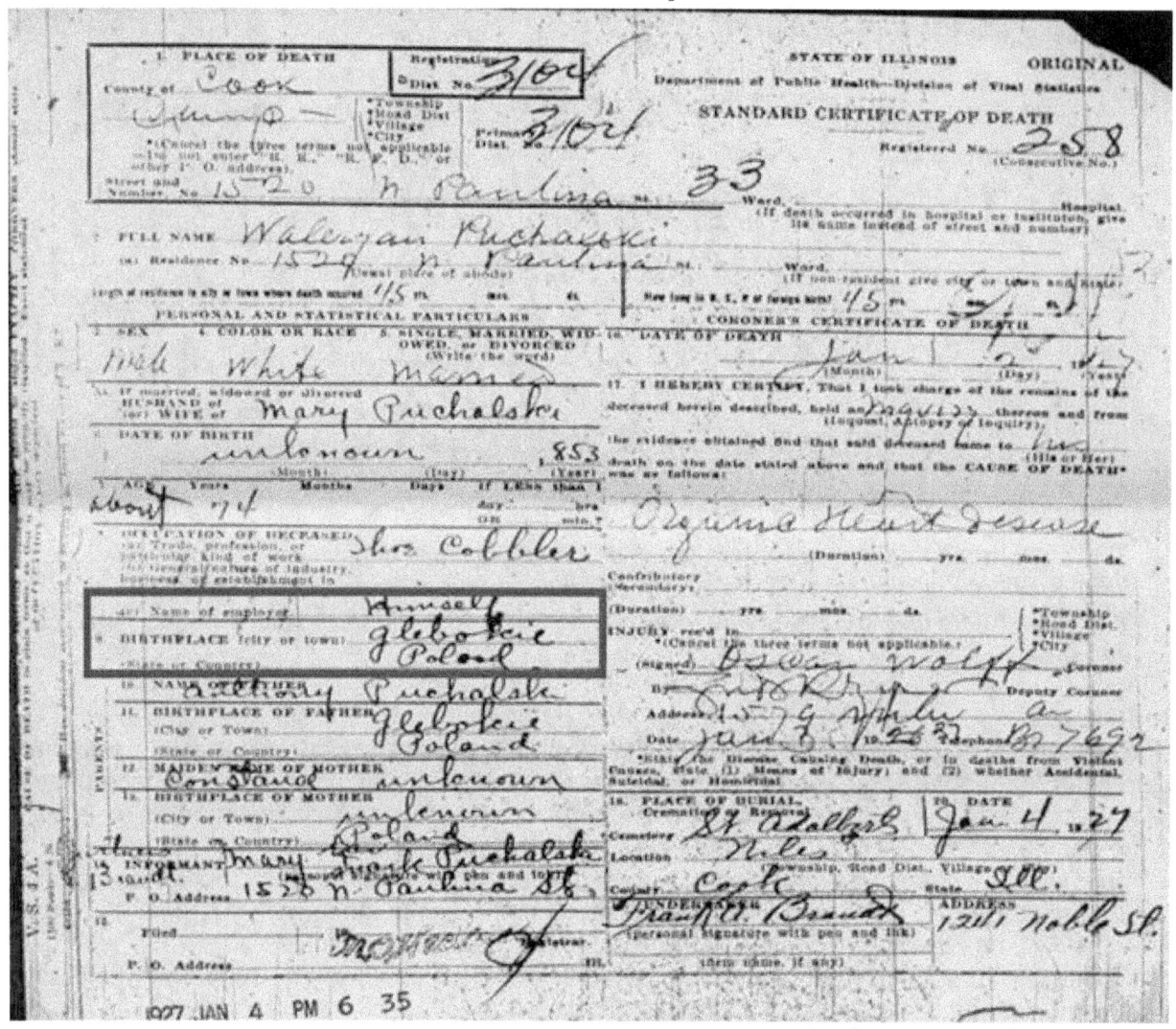

Below is the death certificate for Elizabeth Szabados, my grandmother. Her birthplace is listed as Erdo Hegy, Hungary which was given accurately by her husband Erwin Szabados. Although my grandparents met after they immigrated, Erdo Hegy is located near where my grandfather was born. He would have been familiar with the town and should have been able to give an accurate place of birth for his wife.

Death certificate for Elizabeth Szabados

Obituaries

Many obituaries give only the name of the person who died, the names of their spouse and children and other surviving members of his family.

Occasionally some families give many more details. A more detailed obituary is a good source for information about a person. It gives the name of the deceased and the death or burial date. It may also contain information such as the birth date, place of birth, marriage date, names of parents and spouse, children, occupation, education, and the location of living family members at the time the obituary was written.

Below are three obituaries that list where the decedent was born in the old country. Two of them list when they arrived in the United States.

Below is the obituary for my great-grandmother Josephine Szabados. The information was given to the funeral director by her daughter who was born in America. Also attending the funeral, were her two sons who were born in Hungary and another daughter who was born in America. Josephine's marriage record listed Apatin as her birthplace but her children did not have the marriage record and assumed Pankota was her birthplace because this was the last residence before emigration and the two sons believed they were born in Pankota.

Obituary for My grandmother Josephine Szabados

Bloomington-Normal Deaths

Mrs. Josephine Szabados

Mrs. Josephine Szabados, 76, of 1308 Northwestern Ave. died in the family residence at 2:30 p. m. Wednesday after an illness of two months.

She was taken to the Carmody Funeral Home and will be returned to the residence Thursday afternoon at four o'clock. Services will be held in the residence at 8:30 a. m. Saturday and in St. Mary's Church at 9 a. m. Burial will be in St. Joseph's Cemetery.

Mrs. Szabados was born March 19. 1877 in Pankota, Hungary, the daughter of John and Suzanne Zerna. She was married to Martin Szabados in 1894 in Hungary and came to the United States and to Bloomington in 1907.

Her husband, two daughters, one brother and seven sisters preceded her in death.

Surviving children are Ervin of Roodhouse, Fred of Peoria, Mrs. Marie Westerdahl of 1311 N. Livingston St. and Mrs. Suzanne Myers of 1308 Northwestern Ave. Also surviving are seventeen grandchildren and five great grandchildren. Mrs. Szabados was a member of St. Mary's Church, the St. Anne Society and the Catholic Order of Foresters.

Szabados Funeral

Funeral services for Mrs. Josephine Szabados, 76, of 1308 N. Western Ave., were held at 8:30 a. m. Saturday at the family home and at 9 a. m. at St. Mary's Church. Burial was in St. Joseph's Cemetery. Mrs. Szabados died Wednesday.

The Rev. Fr. Aloys Schweitzer celebrated requiem high mass. The Rev. Fr. John Ring was deacon and the Rev. Fr. Madian Schneider was sub-deacon. Father Schweitzer delivered the funeral sermon and officiated at the graveside.

St. Anne's Society formed an honorary escort. Pallbearers were Martin Szabados, Jesse Szabados, Louis Magy, Martin Deutsch Jr., Joseph Kober and John Szepcsik.

Below is the obituary for Bertha Pohl Lutz who was the great-aunt of my daughter-in-law. The obituary lists her birthplace, immigration plus her living brothers and sisters. Since her brothers and sisters also immigrated as teens or adults, the birthplace that is listed is probably accurate and I have found the town on a map. This is a great obituary for the genealogist because it not only gives her birthplace but it also gives a short history of her life from the time she left Germany, her marriage and includes a list of moves she made with her husband and family.

1942 Obituary for Bertha Pohl Lutz
Obtained from Calhoun County Genealogy Society

Rites for Mrs. Lutz Held Last Saturday

Mrs. Bertha Lutz was born July 1, 1877 at Buchfelde, Province of Posen, Germany. In 1882 the family left the old home and country and came to the United States, where they found a new home at Varna, Ill.

On the 18th day of April, 1895, Bertha Pohl was married to Ernest Lutz, at Winona, Ill. This union was blessed with seven children, of whom two preceded their mother in death. For more than 47 years Mr. and Mrs. Lutz were permitted to share the joys as well as the toils and care of life together.

They moved to Sheldon, Ia., in 1896, where they lived until 1902, when they moved to Manson. In 1913 the family moved to near Clare and in 1919 to Terril; in 1931 they returned to Manson and made their home in the country northeast of town.

Mrs. Lutz enjoyed good health most of her life, which enabled her to attend to the manifold duties of a faithful wife and mother. Last winter she began to suffer from a complication of ailments, but recovered sufficiently to assume her household duties. About two weeks ago she became seriously ill with heart trouble, yet she overcome this attack sufficiently to be able to leave her bed for a short time. On Wednesday morning of last week she suffered another attack, and fell peacefully asleep that afternoon.

Mrs. Lutz leaves to mourn her departure, her aged husband, three sons, Arthur of Terril, Edward of Manson and George of Barnum, two daughters, Margaret, Mrs. Carl Suhrbier of Pocahontas and Irene, Mrs. Walter Weber of Dickens, Ia.; 14 grandchildren, three great-grandchildren, two brothers, Gustave Pohl of Jeffers, Minn., and Adalph Pohl of Rolfe, Iowa.

The funeral service was held at Williams Funeral home on Saturday, June 6, with the Rev. W. E. F. Meier officiating, and the body laid to rest in Roes Hill cemetery.

The obituary shown in the next illustration is the obituary for Josef Joza from the Czech language newspaper Denni Hlasatel. It listed his birthplace as Cerma near Susice in Bohemia (Čechy). There are a number of towns with the name of Cermna but only one near the town of Susice. This is a great obituary for the genealogist because it also lists Josef's parents and siblings plus the family members of his wife.

Obituary for Josef Joza - panel
From Denni Hlasatel February 22, 1912

Oznámení úmrtí,

(Hlubokým žalem sklíčeni a se srdcem zarmouceným oznamujeme truchlivou zprávu všem milým přátelům a známým, že zemřel náš vroucně milovaný manžel, otec, bratr a švagr,

JOSEF JOZA

po krátké nemoci dne 20. února, 1912, o 10. hod. večer v stáří 35 roků. Zesnulý byl rozen v Čermá, okres Sušice v Čechách. Příslušel ku Dvoru sv. Norberta, čís. 637 K. L. Pohřeb drahého zesnulého odbývati se bude v pátek, dne 23. února z domu smutku, 2649 Spaulding ave. o 9. hod. ráno do chrámu Páně sv. Lidmily a odtud na Česko-národní hřbitov. Za tichou soustrast prosí:

JULIE JOZOVÁ, truchlící manželka.

Václav, Marie, Julie, Helena a Josefa, ditky; Vojtěch a Marie Jozovi, rodiče v Čechách; Štěpán Joza, bratr v Čechách; Marie Kříž, Magdalena Jarošík, Josefa Kopecent, Ludmila Bureal, sestry zde; František Kříž, August Jarošík, Petr Kopecent, Jakub Bureal, František a Vilém Syrovátkové a Emanuel Horák, švagři; Marie Syrovátková a Josefa Horáková, švegruše; Václav a Josefa Syrovátkovi, tchán a tchýně.

Kdo by se chtěl pohřbu súčastniti, nechť se přihlásí v domě smutku aneb u pohrobníka p. Jana Jány na Albany ave. nejdále ve čtvrtek do 6 hodin večer.

Ordering a death certificate

To order a death certificate or find an obituary, you will need to know when your ancestor and their relatives died. Listed below are sources that may tell you when your ancestor died.

- **Social Security death index**
  The Social Security Act of 1933 required all employees to register with the Social Security Administration and to contribute along with their employers to the Social Security Fund. If they received any benefits before they died their death would be reported to the Social Security registration to stop the benefits and their death would be listed in the Social Security Death Index (SSDI). The SSDI can be searched at a number of sites online but I have found that Ancestry.com and Familysearch.org have been very useful.

- **State death indexes**
  If your ancestors are not listed in the SSDI, you may find them in a state death index that is based on death certificates that were recorded in state or county records. Some of these indexes may be found online at Ancestry.com and Familysearch.org. Also some states such as Missouri, Illinois, Wisconsin, Michigan, Minnesota, North Dakota, Ohio and Washington have their own websites with death indexes. The next illustration is shown the Website for Minnesota deaths between 1904 and 2001.

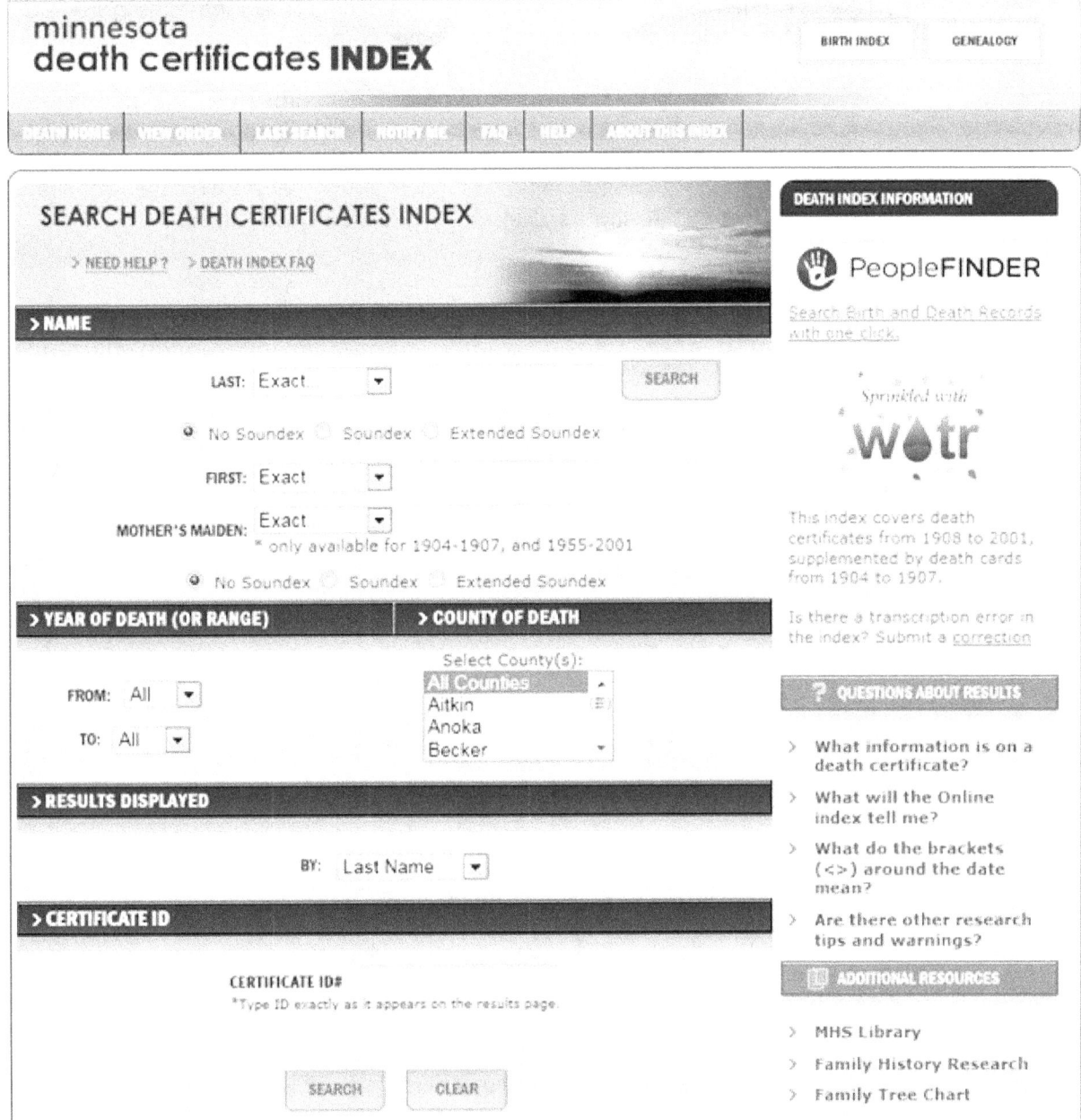

- **Death indexes listed on Ancestry.com** – Ancestry has death indexes for many states and also many indexes for churches and counties in the databases that they offer.
- **Death indexes listed on Familysearch.org** – Familysearch are digitizing and indexing their films and have many death records already uploaded with continuing plans to add more. Check this website regularly as they add databases monthly.

Other sources for death information are cemetery records, gravestone inscriptions, cemetery books and funeral cards.

Cemetery records and grave stones

If you know the cemetery where your ancestors were buried, a trip to the cemetery should give you the date or at least the year of death by viewing the grave marker. Before you try to find the grave site, visit the cemetery office to obtain the location of the grave and a map of the cemetery – the person in the office may be able to mark the location on the map. If you live too far away from the cemetery to visit, you may be able to call the cemetery office and get the date of burial. If the name of the cemetery is not known, searching a number of cemeteries near where your ancestor lived may locate the grave site but will be more time consuming. Many local genealogy societies have compiled cemetery books that list all burials by cemetery and will hopefully list your ancestor. The books will list the information on the grave marker and sometimes volunteers also include the names of parents and other information listed on the death certificate. The next illustration shows a sample page from a cemetery book. Note the extra information listed about relationships plus the listing of parents in some cases.

Sample page from St Joseph's Cemetery, Bloomington, Illinois

```
ST. JOSEPH'S CEMETERY PAGE- 41
CS    KERNER      Frank      no dates              hus. of Josephine
                  Josephine (Mayer)  Feb. 16, 1868 - July 9, 1936
                     wife of Frank
                     dau. of Joseph MAYER
                  Theresa  (Kerner) FOLKS
SS                FRANK    May 21, 1903 -                hus. of Eva
                  Eva (Hirsch)  Dec. 24, 1903 -
                     wife of Frank
                  Frank J.   Dec. 7, 1931 - Dec. 14, 1973
                     Ill. EN2 US Navy Korea
                     son of Frank & Eva   ( Hirsch)
CS                Katherina (Kerner) HOFFMAN
SS                Lena (Kerner) MAYER
CS                Simon  Feb. 21, 1860 -Jan. 26, 1950    hus. of Theresa
                     son of John & Magdalena (Mueller)
                  Theresa (Takaes)  May 17, 1863 - May 30, 1941
                     wife of Simon
                     dau of Joseph & Theresa (Hubner) TAKAES
                  Simon, Jr.   Oct. 26, 1884 - Oct. 23, 1972  hus. of Magdal
                     son of Simon & Theresa (Takaes)
                  Magdalena (Marksteiner) 1890 -
                     wife of Simon, Jr.
                     dau. of John & Anna (Foote) MARKSTEINER
                  Antoinette J.  1922-
                     dau. of Simon & Magdalena (Marksteiner) Jr.
SS                Rose C. (Kerner) EMERY
                                        hus. of Elizabeth
```

Other sources that can help you find the gravesite for your ancestors are:
- Search cemeteries where other relatives are buried.
- Search Nationwide Gravesite Locator for veterans at gravelocator.cem.va.gov
- Findagrave.com
- Internment.net
- Billiongraves.com

The website shown in the next illustration allows you to search for burial locations of veterans and their family members in VA National Cemeteries, state veterans cemeteries and various other military and Department of Interior cemeteries. The database also includes listings for veterans buried in private cemeteries when the grave is marked with a government grave marker. The Nationwide Gravesite Locator has information from burial records from many sources. The data provided by these sources may contain less information than others.

Grave Locator for Department of Veterans Affairs

To search for burial locations of veterans, please provide the following:

Gravesite Locator

Cemetery: -- All --

search options

Last Name: exact match
(Required)

First Name: exact match

Middle Name: exact match

Month   Year (YYYY)

Date of Birth: /

Date of Death: /   Go

Below is the search results for Michael Hutchings
the minor son of Master Sergeant Robert Hutchings

1. **HUTCHINGS, MICHAEL ROBERT**

   DATE OF BIRTH: 05/06/1948

   DATE OF DEATH: 04/13/1966

   BURIED AT: SECTION X SITE 2940   View Map

   FT. SAM HOUSTON NATIONAL CEMETERY

   1520 HARRY WURZBACH ROAD SAN ANTONIO, TX 78209

   (210) 820-3391

   SON (MINOR CHILD) OF HUTCHINGS, ROBERT WILSON

   MSGT US ARMY

County Genealogy websites sponsored by US Genweb. Many county coordinators and volunteers have transcribed the cemetery records for their county. Go to the home page usgenweb.org to find county websites.

USGENWEB home page

Cemetery Index Page from Schuyler County, Illinois website sponsored by USGENWEB

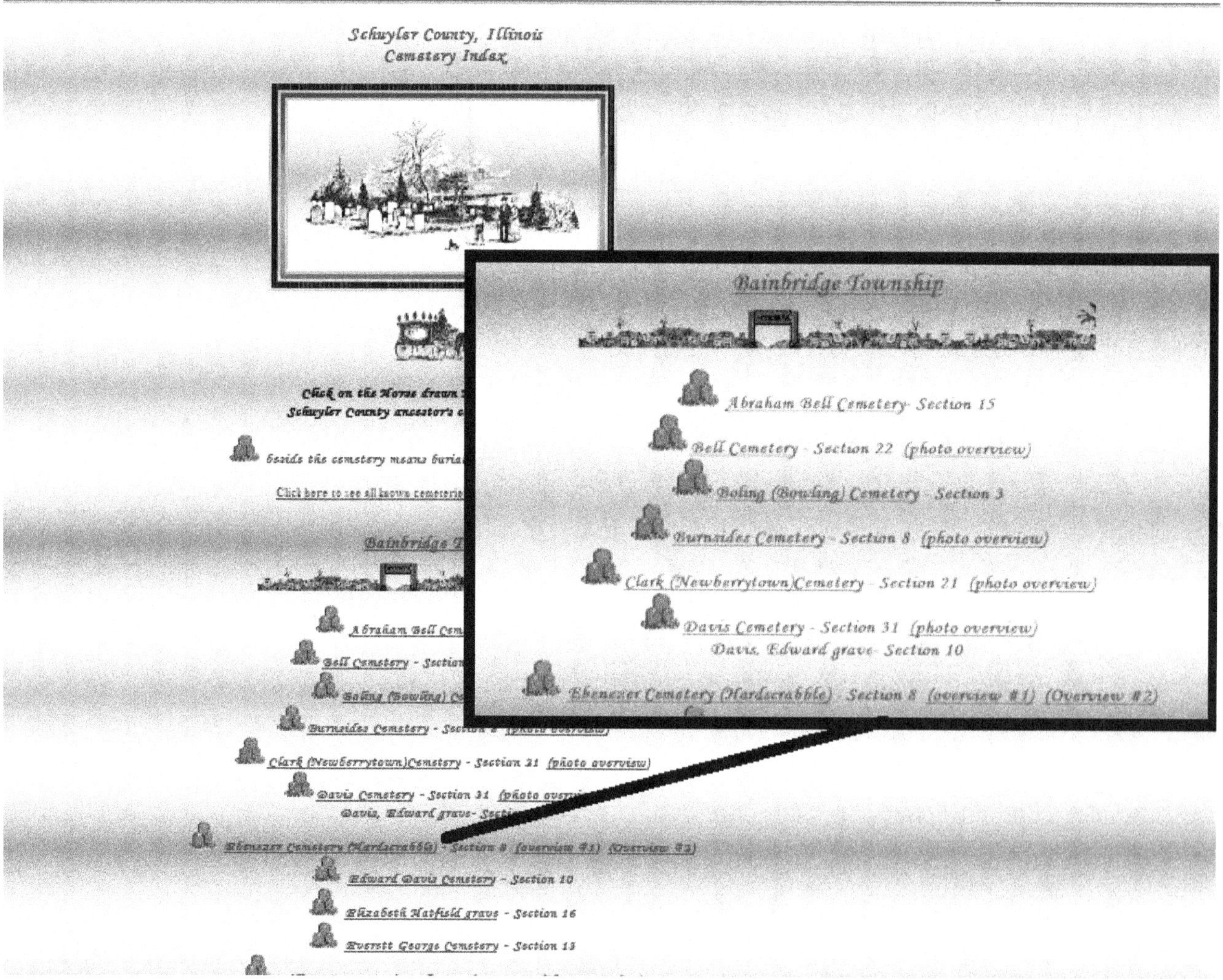

- County Genealogy websites sponsored by Genealogy Trails History Group. Many of these county websites have transcribed the cemetery records for their county. Note that not all county coordinators have been able to upload listings for the cemeteries in their county but you should still try this website to see what is offered. Go to home page genealogytrails.com to find county website.

Portion of the listing of gravestone in Laurel Cemetery in Schuyler County, New York from Genealogytrails web pages

LAUREL HILL CEMETERY

Odessa, Schuyler County, New York

Submitted by Peggy Thompson

NAME	BIRTH DATE	DEATH DATE
Archibald, Adelia	September 9, 1839	1919
Archibald, Fanny	December 1819	1904
Archibald, Walter	1815	1872
Barbery, Robert N. Sgt.	August 27, 1943	January 29, 1968
Brown, Dana Lawrence	January 20, 1951	July 30, 1999
Brown, Lawrence Alva	1914	December 18, 1961
Cure, James Montgomery	October 29, 1807	January 10, 1894
Gulyas, Virginia Koellner	August 9, 1925	January 3, 1998
Hayes, Richard LeRoy		May 12, 1990
Koellner, Charles	August 26, 1900	July 1983
Koellner, Marie A. Rogers	October 31, 1900	November 1986
Kohberger, Frances E. Parker	February 22, 1914	April 3, 2007
Landon, Lillian Barbara Koellner	May 15, 1923	October 29, 2002
Mallory, Aaron Ebenzer	October 17, 1817	May 12, 1893
Mallory, Alexander	July 27, 1831	April 14, 1904
Mallory, Emily Herrick	1832	July 11, 1922
McCracken, Cynthia D. Smith	1951	September 22, 1996
Ring, John	1846	December 21, 1932

- Search the online database at Findagrave.com. This is a free website where you can search over 67 million grave records. Over 800,000 plus contributors submit new listings, updates, corrections, photographs and virtual flowers daily.

Search Page at Findagrave.com

47

- Search the online database at Internment.net. This is a free website where you can browse the cemetery records by county. The number of records is slowly growing as individuals upload their work. At this time many counties and many cemeteries do not have listings for the gravestones but you should still look at the cemeteries in the county of your ancestor.

The next illustration is the County Index Page for New York on Internrment.net. From Home page select the state you need to search, then from the state page (that your see below) select your county and then browse each cemetery in the county.

- **WPA Historical Records Project**

The Works Progress Administration (WPA) was created in 1935 by the U.S. government to help put people back to work and help the nation out of the depression. The WPA funded many construction projects but also had some programs in the humanities. One of the humanities projects was the Historical Records Survey (HRS) which was responsible for creating the soundex indexes of the federal census which genealogists used heavily before the internet. The HRS also compiled indexes of vital statistics, cemetery interments, school records, military records, maps, newspapers, and the list went on and on. After the WPA was dissolved in 1943, some of the records found their way to the hands of state archives and historical societies. These groups microfilmed, indexed, and made them available for use. However, many records were placed into boxes and stored away. Genealogy groups in some states such as Iowa and Minnesota have made the indexed WPA cemetery records available in searchable online databases. The results of a few other states are available in the film catalog Familysearch.org.

The next illustration shows the home page for the Iowa WPA graves survey. The search boxes show that you can enter the name of your ancestor but the county information is optional. If you know the county you should enter it but if the results do not show your ancestor try again without the county information. Your ancestor may have been buried in a neighboring county.

Iowa's WPA Project web Page

★★IOWA★★ GRAVES SURVEY WPA

WPA - Work Projects Administration
1930's Graves Registration Survey

IAGenWeb Project

| Search | Post-em Notes | WPA History | FAQ | Volunteers | Contact Us | | 1 |

Search 656,154 Genealogy, Family History and Ancestry Records within 82 Iowa Counties.

WPA Record Search... (Enter What You Know)

Last Name: begins with ▼

First Name: begins with ▼

County: -All Online Counties- ▼   Submit

The following Iowa counties have been completely transcribed

Adair	Cass	Emmet	Howard	Mahaska	Pocahontas	Van Buren
Adams	Cedar	Fayette	Jackson	Marion	Polk	Wapello
Allamakee	Cerro Gordo	Floyd	Jefferson	Marshall	Poweshiek	Washington
Audubon	Chickasaw	Franklin	Johnson	Mills	Ringgold	Wayne
Black Hawk	Clarke	Fremont	Jones	Mitchell	Sac	Webster
Boone	Clay	Greene	Keokuk	Monroe	Scott	Winnebago
Bremer	Clayton	Grundy	Kossuth	Montgomery	Shelby	Winneshiek
Buchanan	Crawford	Guthrie	Lee	Muscatine	Sioux	Woodbury
Buena Vista	Davis	Hamilton	Linn	O'Brien	Story	Worth
Butler	Decatur	Hancock	Louisa	Page	Tama	Wright
Calhoun	Delaware	Harrison	Lucas	Palo Alto	Taylor	
Carroll	Dickinson	Henry	Madison	Plymouth	Union	

Counties Not Included

Counties not indexed by the 1930s WPA Graves Registration Project, and thus not included in the database on this web site, include **Appanoose, Benton, Cherokee, Clinton, Dallas, Des Moines, Dubuque, Hardin, Humboldt, Ida, Iowa, Jasper, Lyon, Monona, Osceola, Pottawattamie, and Warren.**

Some graves may never be found

- Some family burial grounds were lost when the land was sold to someone outside the family and the cemetery was not maintained by the new owner. The new owners may have also removed the tombstones and converted the land to another use. Tombstones were also lost because they fell over, they were broken or they were removed to be put to another use such as stepping stones.
- Sometimes church grave yards were also covered over when the church was sold and the land converted to another use. Sometimes the graves were moved to another site but many times they were not because no money was provided to do this. The records may have been transferred to a nearby church of the same denomination but if none existed the records and gravesites were lost.

Funeral cards

A little used source that will produce the date of death and the name of the cemetery would be funeral cards that were circulated at the time of the funeral. If a ceremony was performed in a church the card would also list the name of the church. Sometimes the card would also list the birth date. Funeral cards may be found in personal papers your ancestors and the scrap books of relatives and friends. Be sure to ask all relatives about them. The cards may have been collected and saved by their parents.

Note that the funeral card shown on the right not only lists the date of his death but also the birth date, cemetery and the name of the church. It also shows a stamp for the funeral home. All can be used to find more records and information for your ancestor. Church and funeral home records are a valuable source for genealogical records.

Eternal rest grant unto him O Lord, and let perpetual light shine upon him.

In your Charity
Pray for the repose of the soul of

Louis L. Weinberg

Oct. 25, 1892   March 21, 1984

Funeral Mass Held at
ST. IGNATIUS CHURCH
March 24, 1984   11:00 A.M.

Interment
ALL SAINTS CEMETERY

✝

Absolve we beseech Thee, O Lord, the soul of Thy departed servant that being dead to this world he may live to Thee, and whatever sins he may have committed through human frailty, do Thou, of Thy most merciful goodness forgive, through Jesus Christ Our Lord. Amen.

Our Father. Hail Mary.

JOHN E. MALONEY
FUNERAL HOME

CROCE

Where to Obtain Death Certificates

- State Archives or Genealogy Societies

  In many states, death certificates must be ordered from the State Health Departments. In other states, copies of death certificates can be ordered from county offices. Once you find where your ancestor died, you will be able to find out how to order their death certificate by going to the state or county website. Also, check the websites of the state Genealogical society where your ancestor died to see if they offer copies of death certificates. Some states are also offering digital copies of death certificates that can be downloaded immediately from their websites. Below is shown the search page for Missouri Death Certificates. The websites will show the actual death certificate and will allow a free download of the image.

State of South Dakota Vital Records Order Page

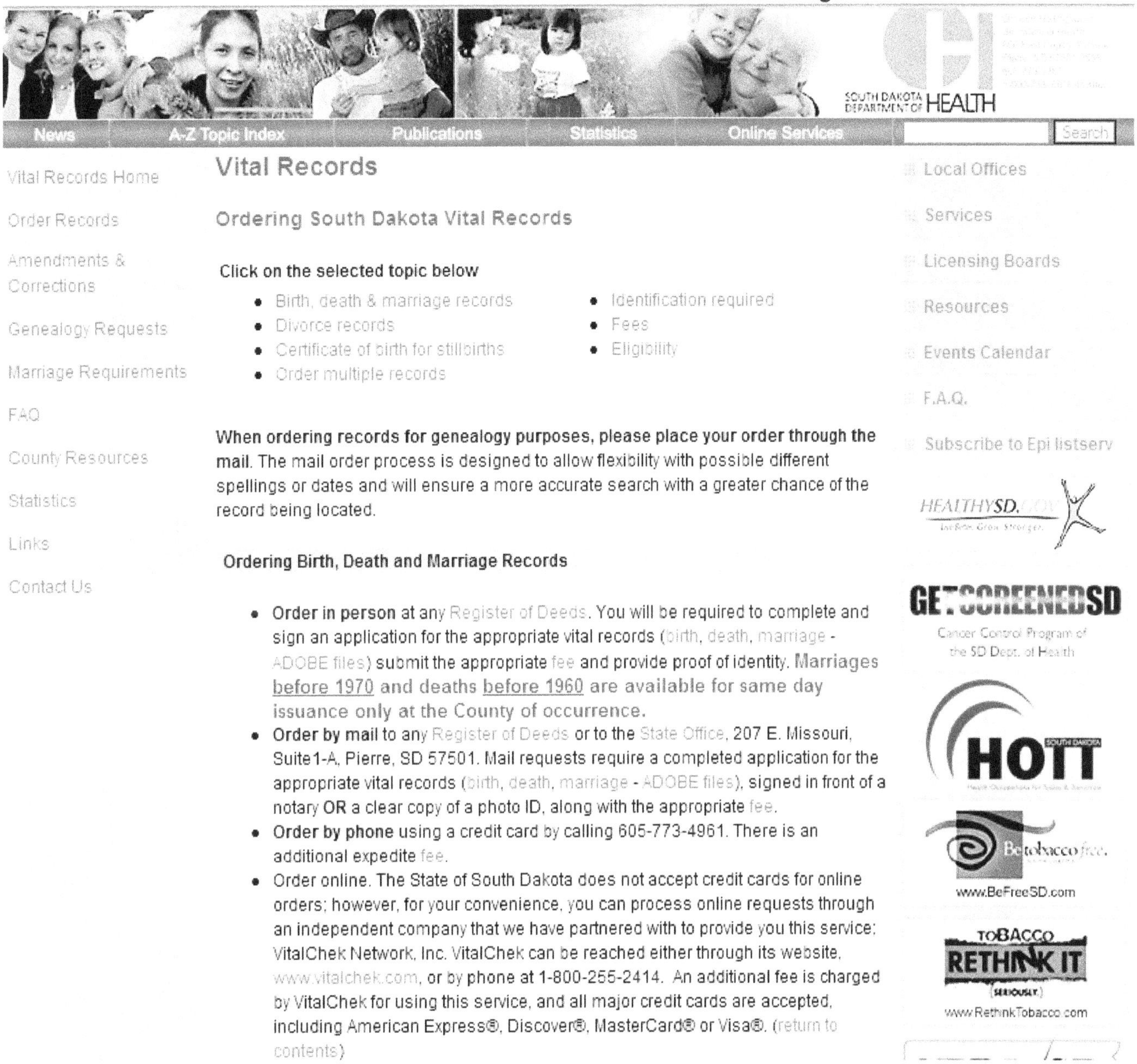

| News | A-Z Topic Index | Publications | Statistics | Online Services | Search |

Vital Records

Vital Records Home

Order Records

Amendments & Corrections

Genealogy Requests

Marriage Requirements

FAQ

County Resources

Statistics

Links

Contact Us

Ordering South Dakota Vital Records

Click on the selected topic below

- Birth, death & marriage records
- Divorce records
- Certificate of birth for stillbirths
- Order multiple records
- Identification required
- Fees
- Eligibility

When ordering records for genealogy purposes, please place your order through the mail. The mail order process is designed to allow flexibility with possible different spellings or dates and will ensure a more accurate search with a greater chance of the record being located.

Ordering Birth, Death and Marriage Records

- **Order in person** at any Register of Deeds. You will be required to complete and sign an application for the appropriate vital records (birth, death, marriage - ADOBE files) submit the appropriate fee and provide proof of identity. Marriages before 1970 and deaths before 1960 are available for same day issuance only at the County of occurrence.
- **Order by mail** to any Register of Deeds or to the State Office, 207 E. Missouri, Suite 1-A, Pierre, SD 57501. Mail requests require a completed application for the appropriate vital records (birth, death, marriage - ADOBE files), signed in front of a notary OR a clear copy of a photo ID, along with the appropriate fee.
- **Order by phone** using a credit card by calling 605-773-4961. There is an additional expedite fee.
- Order online. The State of South Dakota does not accept credit cards for online orders; however, for your convenience, you can process online requests through an independent company that we have partnered with to provide you this service: VitalChek Network, Inc. VitalChek can be reached either through its website, www.vitalchek.com, or by phone at 1-800-255-2414. An additional fee is charged by VitalChek for using this service, and all major credit cards are accepted, including American Express®, Discover®, MasterCard® or Visa®. (return to contents)

Local Offices

Services

Licensing Boards

Resources

Events Calendar

F.A.Q.

Subscribe to Epi listserv

Illinois State Genealogy Society (ISGS) order page

 STATE GENEALOGICAL SOCIETY

Home

About ISGS

Join ISGS!

Members
Section

ISGS
Webinars

Shop and
Support
ISGS

Calendar of
Events

ISGS
Projects

ISGS
Services

Death
Certificate
Lookup

Genealogy
Committee

Education
Committee

ISGS
Newsletter

ISGS
Publications

Forms

Links

Illinois
Resources

Surname
Research

Free
Databases

Death Certificate Lookup

ISGS has established this service to assist members and researchers who do not have easy access to the Illinois State Archives to obtain death certificate copies. Cost per certificate is $6.00 for ISGS members and $10.00 for non-members. You may send as many requests at the same time as you wish.

To obtain non-certified copies of death certificates from the 1916-1947 timeframe, please follow these steps

- Go to the Illinois State Archives Death Certificate Index (link opens in new window)

- Search for the individual death certificate(s) you want.

- After you find the correct certificates(s), print or copy down the information exactly as displayed on your screen.

- Order Online - If you would like to order online using a MasterCard, Visa, Discover, American Express or a PayPal account, you can use our shopping cart below. Your information is kept safe and secure by the PayPal payment service.

- Order by Mail - If you would prefer to mail your request, print out the ISGS Death Certificate Request Form and transfer the death certificate information to the form. Mail the form along with your check made payable to the Illinois State Genealogy Society to the address shown on the form. (Note: Credit cards are only available online.)

If you have any questions, email isgsoffice@ilgensoc.org.

Illinois State Genealogical Society Membership		
	Individual - $30.00	ADD
	Joint - $35.00	ADD
ISGS members receive a 40% discount on certificates. Not a member? Join ISGS now and start saving immediately!	Canadian - $35.00	ADD
	International (Outside U.S./Canada) - $65.00	ADD

Copies of 1916-1947 Death Certificate
(Death Certificates filed before 1916 and after 1947 are not currently available)

Select Certificate Fee

○ ISGS Member - $6.00   ○ Non-Member - $10.00

Enter Death Certificate Information

Last Name: _____	First Name: _____	Middle Name: _____
Sex/Race: ___ Age: ___	Certificate #: _____	Death Date: _____
County: Select County ▼	City: _____	Date Filed: _____

ADD

The illustration below is of the search page for downloading Missouri death certificates 1910- 1961.

Missouri Death Certificate search page

Missouri Digital Heritage   Collections   Death Certificates

MISSOURI STATE ARCHIVES
Missouri Death Certificates

Death certificates contain valuable information for family historians and researchers. The Missouri Death Certificate Database, containing death records created after 1910 and over 50 years old, makes that information available online through a searchable index that links to a digitized image of the original death certificate.

The index can be searched by first name and last name, county, and by year and month. Once a name is selected, a digitized image of the original certificate can be retrieved.

This is an ongoing project and additional records will be added as they are transcribed and imaged. If the image of the certificate is not yet available researchers can request a photocopy of the certificate by contacting the Archives Reference Desk. For death certificates less than 50 years old please contact the Missouri Bureau of Vital Records

If you have questions or comments about these records, please contact the Missouri State Archives at archref@sos.mo.gov

For more information:

Missouri Birth and Death Records A Brief History
Death Certificate Project
Death Certificate Request Form
Reporting Corrections
Dictionary of Medical Terms

For additional resources:

Missouri State Archives Pre-1910 Missouri Birth and Death Records Database
Missouri Bureau of Vital Records
State Historical Society of Missouri Newspaper Search Births Death and Marriages

Search Death Certificate Index

Last Name: First Name:

County: - Search All -   ▼   Year:

[Search] [Clear]   Images are available for: 1910 – 1960

Advanced Search

- **Family History Centers films**
  Death certificates are available on Family History Center films available on Famlysearch.org. Generally they are listed under the subject of vital records along with birth and marriage records. They will also be listed by county in date order.

**Webpage at Familysearch.org describing the
Illinois Death Certificates available on FHC Films**

FAMILYSEARCH   Learn   FamilySearch Centers   Indexing   Blog

🖨 Print

Death certificates for the state of Illinois, 1916-1945, excluding Chicago with the exception of stillbirths; index, 1916-1938; internet index, 1916-1950

« Back to search results

	authors:	Illinois. Public Board of Health. Archives. (Main Author)
	format:	Manuscript/On Film
	language:	English
View this publication online	publications:	Salt Lake City, Utah : Filmed by the Genealogical Society of Utah, 1988-1992
	physical:	684 microfilm reels, 16 mm.
	references:	(Related (rev) Hard copy of library catalog record for death certificates for the state of Illinois, 1916-1945, excluding Chicago with the exception of stillbirths

**Webpage at Familysearch.org showing some of the
film numbers available for Illinois Death Certificates**

Film Notes

Note	Location	Film
INDEX. 1916-1938. Full name, alphabetical on 191 microfiches.	FHL US/CAN Fiche	6016862
[1916 Deaths] ADAMS County, Illinois-BOND County, Illinois, certificate nos. 1-1501	FHL US/CAN Film	1530531
[1916 Deaths] BOND County, Illinois-COLES County, Illinois, certificate nos. 1502-4375	FHL US/CAN Film	1530532
[1916 Deaths] COLES County, Illinois-COOK County, Illinois, certificate nos. 4375-6938	FHL US/CAN Film	1530530
[1916 Deaths] COOK County, Illinois-CUMBERLAND County, Illinois, certificate nos. 6939-9409	FHL US/CAN Film	1531026

- **County Clerks or Health Departments**
  Some states may allow you to order death certificates from the county clerk or health department. Check both State and county websites to see which is available. The next illustration is the web page of the McLean County, Illinois Health Departments vital records order page as an example.

Web   page   to   order   Death   certificate   from   McLean   County   Health   Department

Where to find Obituaries
- **Online newspaper banks**
  There are many newspapers that have been digitized and are available online. In most cases their pages are available online - both news stories and obituaries. Most of these records are available at subscription websites but some are also available on your local library's online databases.

  Online Newspaper Archives websites are:
  - Newspaperarchive - http://www.newspaperarchive.com/
  - NewsBank - http://www.newsbank.com/
  - Genealogy Bank - http://www.genealogybank.com/gbnk/
  - ProQuest - http://www.proquest.com/
  - Footnote – http://Footnote.com/
  - Godfrey Memorial Library - http://www.godfrey.org/

  You may also need to search the online archives for a small local paper that is not included on any of the large online databases. Go to their online website to do this search.

  Below is the search page for one of the online databases – NewsBank which offers obituaries from all states. This particular site offers options to select specific states and specific papers to limit your search and produce narrow search results. Most results for obituaries will be in a text format but some may be pictures of the newspaper pages.

Search page for NewsBank Obituaries available at many libraries

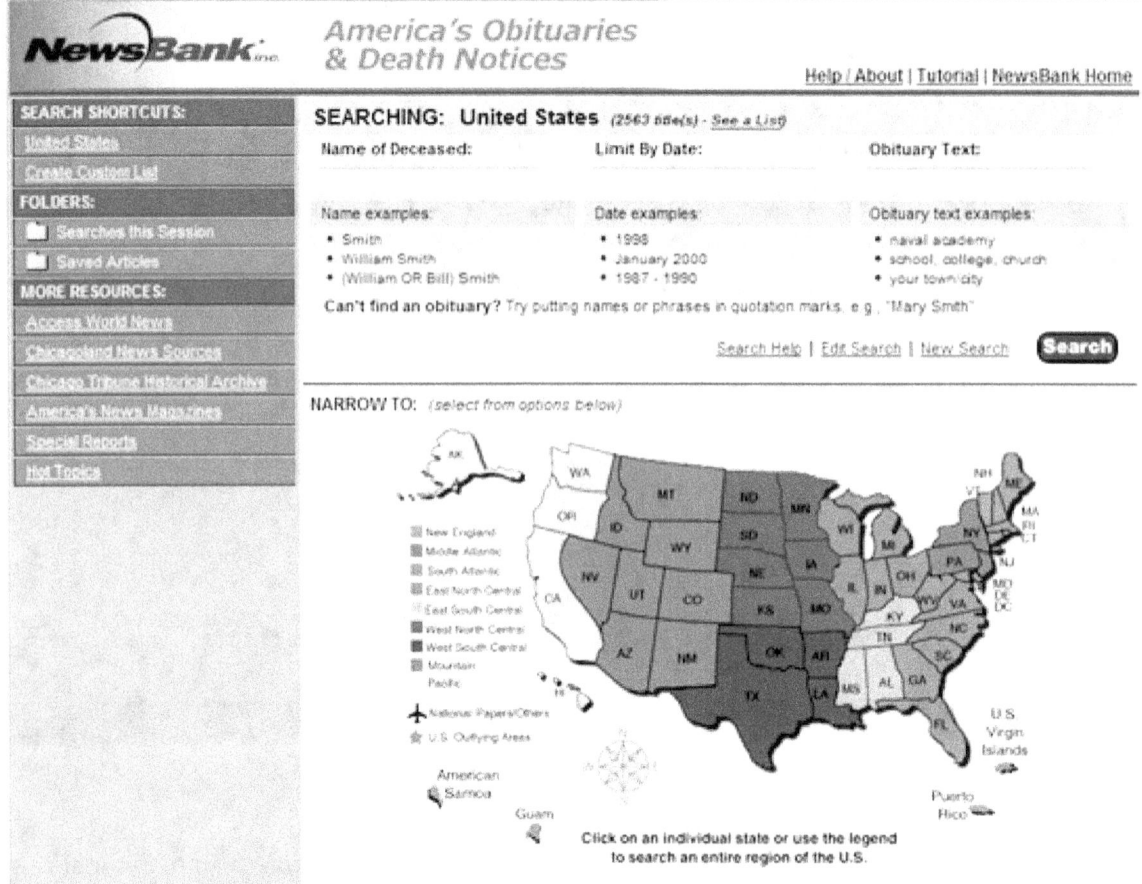

- **Local genealogy or historical society collections**
  Some local genealogical or historical societies may also have collections of obituaries that they have cutout and saved from their local papers. Societies may save these files at their local meeting room, their local library or their local historical museum. If their location is nearby you will find a visit will be very interesting. However, if their location is too distant for a day-trip, call, write or email them to find out what they have. If your list is small they will probably search their files and sent copies for a nominal fee or request for a donation.

Summary for Death records
1. Death certificates and obituaries may list place of birth
2. Towns listed on death records may be inaccurate but still should be used as clues.
3. To obtain a copy of the death certificate and obituary you will need to know when they died
4. Copies of the death certificate may be obtained from county offices and sometimes online
5. Copies of obituaries may be found on the internet at online news banks and also from local genealogical societies.

7 FINDING YOUR IMMIGRANT ANCESTORS

Passenger Manifests

The story of the arrival in America of your ancestors was an important event for your family. Their arrival and the arrival of the many immigrants that came before and after them are a large part of American history. Most U.S. citizens are descendants of immigrants and these immigrants contributed to the tremendous growth America enjoyed in its early years in Virginia and New England to the post World War II housing boom. The industrial growth in the 1900s could not have happened without the immigrants. Your immigrant ancestors were a part of this history. Passenger manifests from the ships help document the arrival of your ancestors and may give you valuable information of where they left and where they were going in America. Finding the passenger manifest will also answer the important question of whether they were traveling alone, with their family, with relatives or with friends.

Immigrants arriving at Ellis Island

The Steerage Act of 1819 required the captain or master of all ships arriving in America to deliver a passenger manifest to a federal official. This was the first time the federal government required the documentation of the arrival of immigrants. For arrivals prior to the steerage act, genealogists have to rely on finding lists generated from the ships' logs. Early formats for the passenger manifest that were used after the Steerage Act listed the passenger's name, age, gender, occupation, what country they left and what country was their destination.

After 1893, formats were gradually expanded and in late 1907 they became two pages. This larger format listed marital status, last residence, the ability to read or write, final destination in the U.S., name of friend or relative in the U.S., the name of relative where they left, mother tongue, if they had been in the U.S. prior, physical description and birthplace.

Some passenger manifests will list one to four town names depending on the year of immigration. I have found that the town names listed have been very helpful in my research but the spelling of the names usually have problems. Most immigrants were illiterate so their information may have been entered on the document phonetically. This led to many misspellings but remembering that the names may have been written phonetically should still prove helpful.

Different Passenger Manifest Formats
The format of the passenger manifests that US immigration officials required changed over the years.

Below is a review of when and where town names were listed on passenger manifest:
- Pre- 1890: column lists what country they left (occasionally an area or town was also listed)

- Before 1906: column 10 lists the last residence of the immigrant

- 1906 & 1907: Birthplace is listed in the far right column, the last residence of the immigrant is listed in column 10

- 1908 & after: This format has two pages - birthplace is listed in the far right column on the second page, column 10 lists the last residence of the immigrant, column 11 lists a relative they left and where that relative lived

The following illustrations are examples of each format.

Pre- 1890

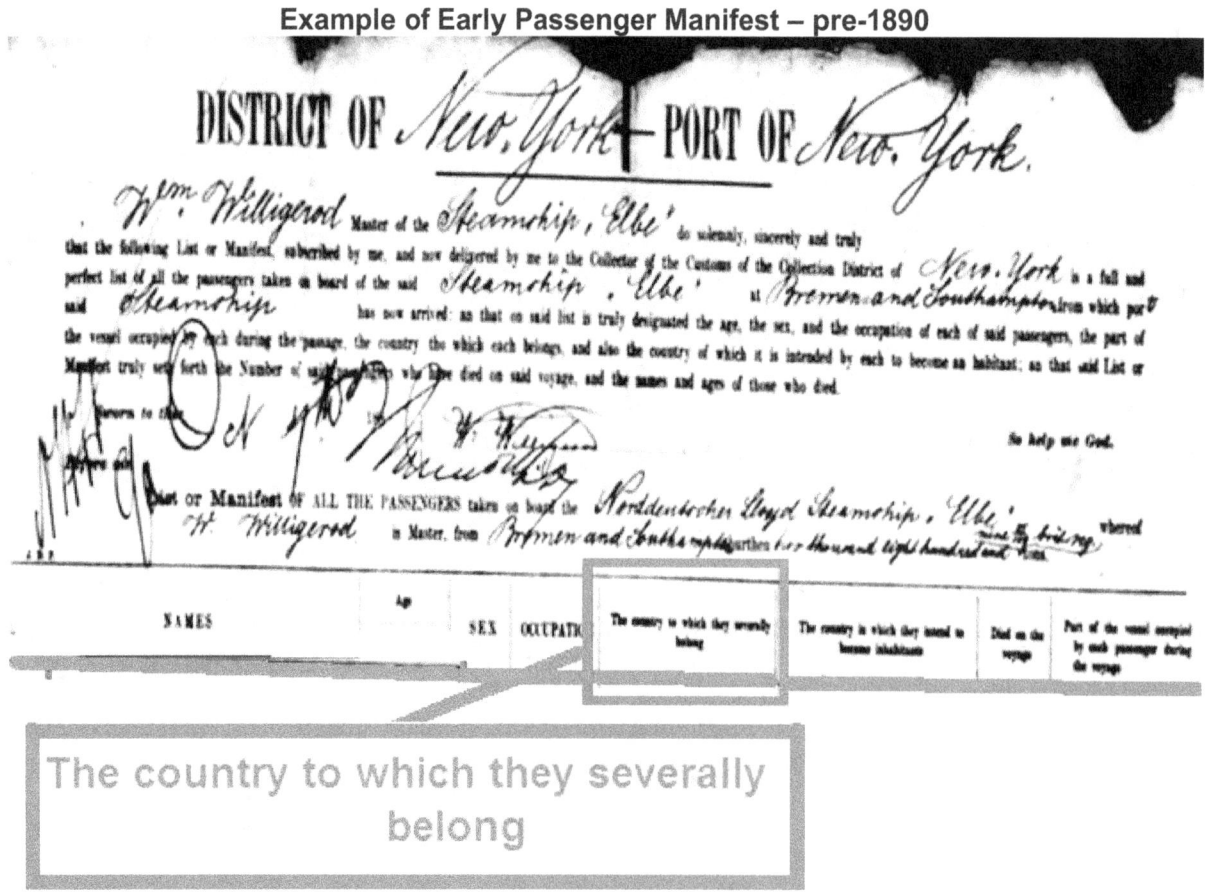

Example of Early Passenger Manifest – pre-1890

The country to which they severally belong

1893 and 1902
Questions listed on manifests between 1893 and 1902 included - name, age, gender, married or single, occupation, read and write, nationality, last residence, final destination, have ticket to last destination, who paid for passage, amount of cash, in U.S. before, person and address at final destination, ever in prison, polygamist, anarchist, health, deformed or crippled, height. In 1903 the race of people column was added.

Questions listed on manifests before 1893 had many variations. Here are the questions listed on the 1895 passenger manifest in the next illustration - full name, age, gender. married/single, occupation, citizen of which country, native country, destination, citizen of US, transient of staying, class of ticket, number of bags, port of departure, date and cause of death.

1895 Passenger manifest

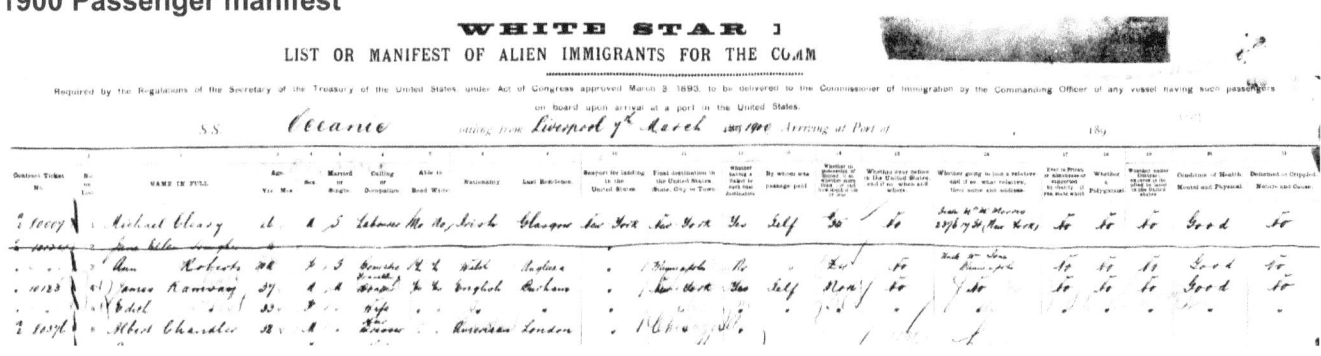

The questions on the 1900 passenger manifest in the next illustration are similar to the 1895 and adds the following - read/write, nationality, last residence, arrival port, destination, who paid for passage, amount of money, in U.S. previously, ever in prison or poorhouse, polygamist, under labor contract, physical and mental condition, deformed or crippled

1900 Passenger manifest

Example of Passenger Manifest Used between 1903 and 1906

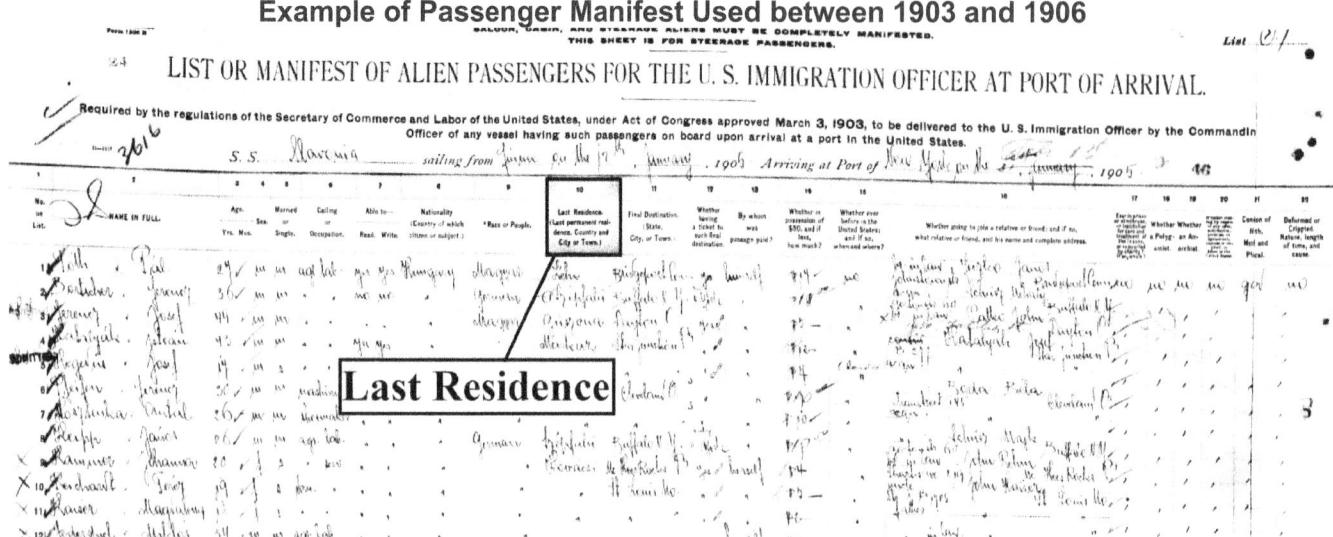

1906 and 1907

Questions listed on 1906 and 1907 manifest format included - name, age, gender, married or single, occupation, read and write, nationality, race or people, last residence, final destination, have ticket to last destination, who paid for passage, amount of cash, in U.S. before, person and address at final destination, ever in prison, polygamist, anarchist, health, deformed or crippled, height, complexion, color of hair and eyes, marks or identification and birthplace.

Passenger Manifest for Martin Szabados
– format used 1906 & 1907

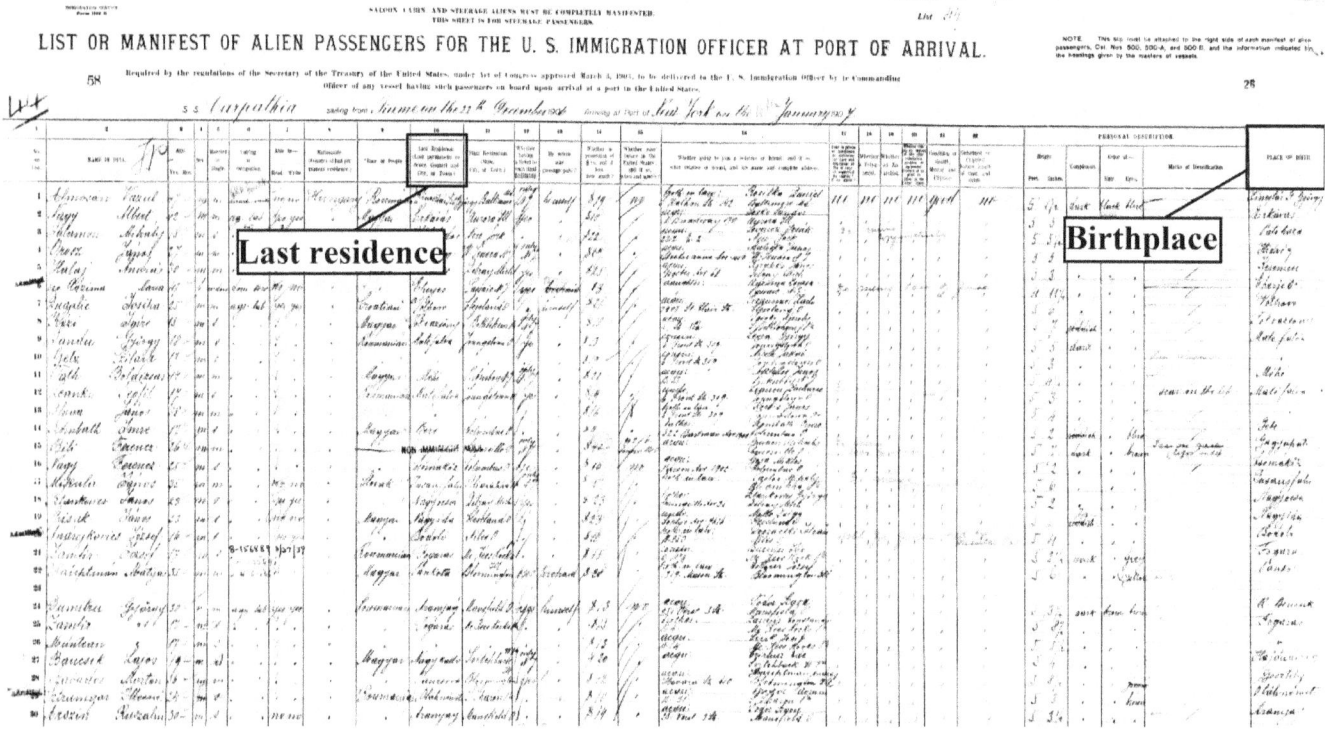

1908 and after

Questions listed on the manifest format in 1908 and after included - name, age, gender, married or single, occupation, read and write, nationality, race or people, last residence, who they left and where did they leave, final destination, have ticket to last destination, who paid for passage, amount of cash, in U.S. before and where, person and address at final destination, ever in prison, polygamist, anarchist, health, deformed or crippled, height, complexion, color of hair and eyes, marks or identification and birthplace.

Example of Passenger Manifest 1908 & after - left side of page

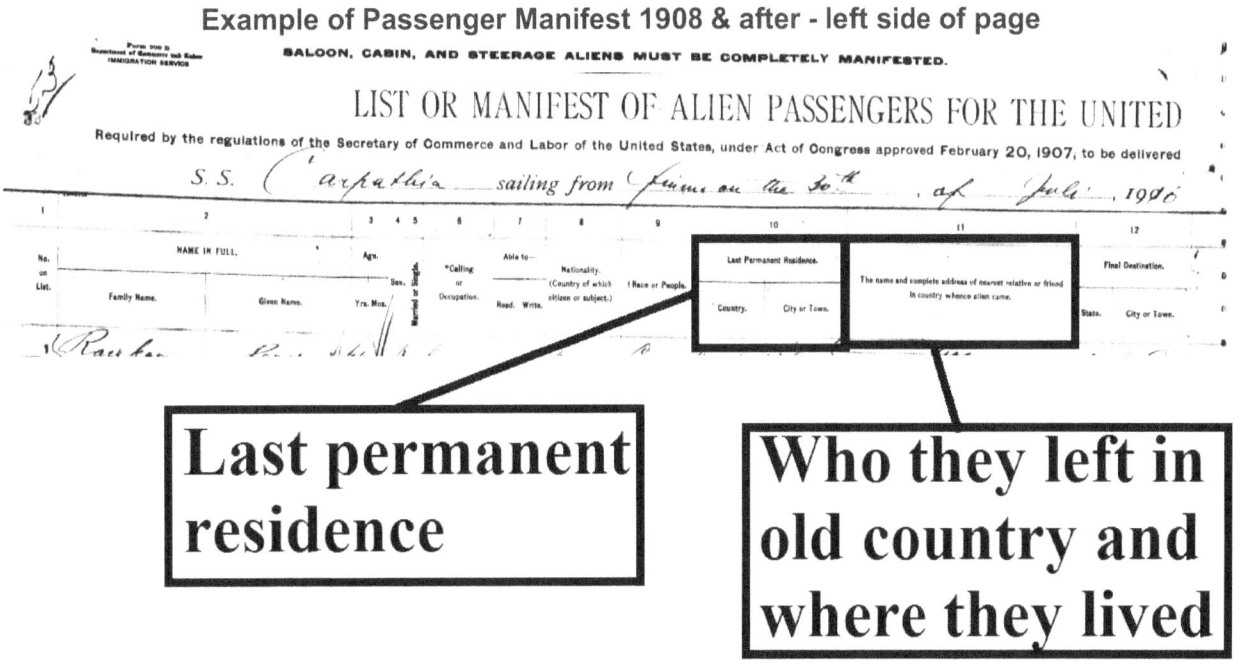

Example of Passenger Manifest 1908 & after - right side of page

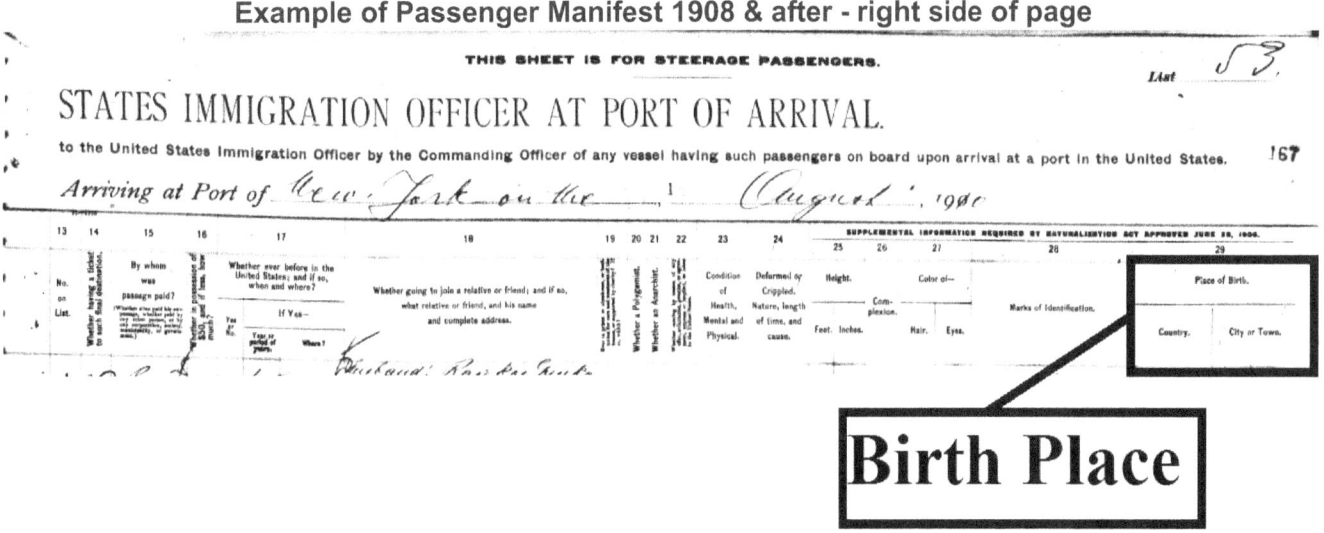

Please remember that most of the information listed on the passenger records are not primary and may contain errors. However they should be used as clues to find other documents and many facts such as the name of the ship, where they left, where and when they arrived and who arrived with them can add rich facts to your family history.

Where did they arrive?

Between 1820 and 1920 almost 30 million immigrants entered the U.S. through over thirteen ports. The most immigrants entered through New York with about 24 million - this included numbers from Castle Gardens and then Ellis Island. Boston with 2.1 million was next and was followed by Baltimore with 1.5 million and Philadelphia with 1.2 million immigrants.

Searching

Before you begin to search for your passenger manifest, you should have a number of facts available.

One fact that you must know is your ancestor's full original name - both given and surname. Since many European names were changed after arrival, finding your ancestor's full original name may be a challenge. Some documents that may list your ancestor's full original names are - their exit documents if they were saved, church records for their marriage and the birth of their children, family bibles and old letters

The myth of name changes

Many family oral histories believe that family names were changed when immigrants entered America. However, this is a myth. Names on passenger manifests were based on official documents presented by the immigrant to the ship line at the time of boarding. It would be illegal to change their names. Also, immigration stations were staffed with large numbers of translators to help insure the information that was given by the immigrants was recorded accurately. If families changed the spelling of their surnames, they did it after arrival and this was usually due to daily problems in its use and to make it easier for the people around them to pronounce their name.

Name variations and spelling

Some instances of variations in names found on passenger manifests may be have been caused when the ship's purser did not use the immigrant's documents as prescribed. Instead he wrote the name on the manifest from questions he asked the immigrant. The immigrant may have been able to recognize their name written in the Cyrillic alphabet or in Hebrew but could not correct the manifest if the purser wrote the name phonetically in the Latin alphabet. The immigrant may not have caught the error of the purser writing the immigrant's name incorrectly because they were illiterate.

Remembering that your ancestor's name may be listed on the passenger manifest as a variant should help you find your ancestor faster. Use the correct spelling first and if your ancestor is not found, use name variations and wild cards. (See chapter nine for an explanation of wild cards). First names are important in your search and many variants of given names could be used. Sometimes it is best to use the part of the given name with wild cards to reduce the problem with the given name variants. I have found two books have useful lists of given name variants - _Foreign Variations and Diminutives of English Names_ by U.S. Department of Justice and _First Names Of The Polish Commonwealth: Origins & Meanings_ by William F. Hoffman. Both books list many given names using a number of foreign languages. Another problem with given names was caused when the immigrant preferred to use their middle name but their exit documents required the purser to list their first name on the passenger manifest.

Two additional facts that your should have to find the passenger manifest of your ancestors are the approximate age at arrival and the approximate year of arrival. Both of these facts may be part of your family oral history. The census records for 1900, 1910, 1920 and 1930 can also be a source to give you clues as when your ancestors arrived. These census records listed the year of arrival and their naturalization status. The years listed on each census record may vary but using a small range of years will still help you narrow your search. Naturalization papers from 1906 or after will give the exact year of arriaval and the name of the ship and this information will allow you to find the passenger manifest faster.

The following are description of five of the largest sources for Passenger Manifests.

1. Ellisisland.org (New York arrivals only - 1892 and after

The Ellis Island Immigration Station opened on January 1, 1892 and had three large ships land on the first day with 700 immigrants passing through its gates. Almost 450,000 immigrants were processed at the station during its first year and about 1.5 million immigrants were processed through this immigration station in its first five years in use. However, on June 15, 1897, a fire possibly caused by faulty wiring, turned the wooden structures on Ellis Island into ashes. No losses of life were reported. However most of the immigration records dating back to 1855 were destroyed. The Barge Office was once again used as the immigration station while new fireproof buildings were being built on Ellis Island. The peak year for immigration at Ellis Island was 1907, with 1,004,756 immigrants processed. Note that Ellis Island was the largest and main immigration station but many European immigrants also arrived through the ports of Boston, Philadelphia, Baltimore, New Orleans and Canada. Passenger manifests from these other ports are not available through the Ellis Island website.

Ellis Island Museum

The Statue of Liberty-Ellis Island Foundation (SO LEIF) was founded in 1982 to restore the Statue of Liberty and Ellis Island.

The Foundation, working with its public partner, the National Park Service of the U. S. Department of the Interior, first restored and upgraded the Statue of Liberty. Work on the statue included restoring the outside finish of the statue after almost a century of weathering and pollution plus replacement of her torch and strengthening of her crown's rays. An army of architects, historians, engineers, and almost 1000 laborers also installed new elevators and an informative exhibit in the Statue's base. The July 4th weekend, 1986, saw a gala three-day event celebrating the restoration.

The Foundation then turned its attention to the restoration of Ellis Island--the largest historical restoration in the history of the United States. The buildings of Ellis Island had sadly deteriorated over the years. When the Island re-opened in September of 1990--two years ahead of schedule-- it unveiled the world-class Ellis Island Immigration Museum, where some rooms appeared as they had during the height of immigrant processing. Other areas housed theaters, libraries, an oral history recording studio, and exhibits on the immigration experience. In the 1990s, the Foundation restored two more buildings (for a total of 5 buildings saved and restored on Ellis Island), expanding and upgrading the Museum Library and Oral History Studio, and creating a Children's Orientation Center and the Ellis Island Living Theatre. The Ellis Island Immigration Museum has welcomed nearly 40 million visitors since its opening in 1990.

Working to promote knowledge of the Island, the Statue, and immigration history, the Foundation has also published and made available to libraries and schools many books and curriculum guides, as well as a CD-ROM produced in collaboration with the History Channel.

The Foundation's current project is a significant expansion of the Ellis Island Immigration Museum to be called The Peopling of America® Center. The Center will enlarge the story currently told of the Ellis Island Era (1892-1954) to include the entire panorama of the American immigration experience from this country's earliest days right up to the present. It is expected to be completed in 2012.

Passenger records for immigrants who were processed at Ellis Island are available for search and viewing at http://www.ellisisland.org/. The site states over 25 million records are available for viewing. To search, you are required to register but a subscription is not required. Digital copies of the actual years are available for viewing. However, there are no options available to download a digital copy although you should be able to do a screen print to save a copy. An 8 ½ x 11 archival quality certificate can be ordered from the Foundation for $29 and you may also order an 11 x 17 copy of each page for $29 per page or an 11 x 22 copy for $39 per page.

2. CastleGarden.org - index covering New York arrivals up to 1891
Castle Garden was New York's first immigration station and it predated Ellis Island. It had more than 8 million people arrived through it's from 1855 to 1890.

Castle Garden – ca 1880

The Battery Conservancy created CastleGarden.org as an educational project. This is a free site that offers access to an extraordinary database of information on 11 million immigrants from 1820 through 1892. The site offers indexes and extractions of the information from the passenger manifests but does not offer digital copies of the actual documents. The next illustration is an example of a page that shows the details available from the Castle Garden website. I have used the Castle Garden website to find the arrival information for some of my ancestors that I could not find on other internet databases. When you search using only the surname and a narrow range for the arrival year, the results will show results are sorted by arrival date and family groupings will be listed together. This has allowed me to identify the arrival of the families even though the names may be spelled differently. I then used the arrival information to find the digital copy of the document on Ancestry.com.

Sample page from CastleGarden.org

CHRISTIAN SCHULTZ			
FIRST NAME	CHRISTIAN	RELATIVE LEFT BEHIND	
LAST NAME	SCHULTZ	NAME OF RELATIVE LEFT BEHIND	
OCCUPATION	SUGAR BAKER	ADDRESS OF RELATIVE LEFT BEHIND	
AGE	23	TICKET	
SEX	Male	PAID BY	Self
LITERACY	Unknown	IN THE US BEFORE	Unknown
SHIP	SIR ROBERT PEEL	IN THE US WHEN	
ARRIVED	10 Mar 1849	IN THE US WHERE	
COUNTRY	SWEDEN	GOING TO SOMEONE IN THE US	Unknown
PORT OF DEPARTURE	LONDON	RELATIONSHIP TO THAT SOMEONE IN THE US	
PLACE OF LAST RESIDENCE	U	NAME OF RELATIVE IN THE US	
PROVINCE OF LAST RESIDENCE	UNKNOWN		
CITY OR VILLAGE OF DESTINATION	UNITED STATES	ADDRESS OF RELATIVE IN THE US	
PLAN	Unknown	CITY OF RELATIVE IN THE US	
PASSAGE	Unknown	COUNTRY OF BIRTH	SWEDEN
MONEY		PLACE OF BIRTH	

3. Local libraries (search by date and ship)
Before passenger records were available online, 35mm films that contained copies of the actual documents were purchased by some libraries to make this information available to their patrons. Each film was organized by date of arrival and by ship but no index of passengers was available. Each film has to be viewed page by page to find the name of your ancestors. These films are now rarely used due to the availability online of their images and because they are searchable online by the immigrants name.

4. Ancestry.com (all ports)
Ancestry.com is a subscription-based genealogy research website with over 5 billion records online and offers the largest selection of digital copies of passenger records. Documents from most ports of entry are available in the Ancestry.com databases. This includes arrivals from the major ports of New York, Philadelphia, Boston and Baltimore but also arrivals from Canadian ports and border crossings. This site can also be accessed at most libraries using Ancestry Library Edition. The following illustration shows the basic search page for Ancestry.com but more detailed search screens are available if specific ports of entry are searched. Digital copies of the actual documents can be saved to your computer from Ancestry.com's databases. If you cannot find your ancestors using simple searches, you may need to use advance search methods by using name variations and wild cards. Also remember that documents were lost in the 1897 fire of the Ellis Island Building and that some documents were damaged due to their age.

Sample search page from Ancestry.com

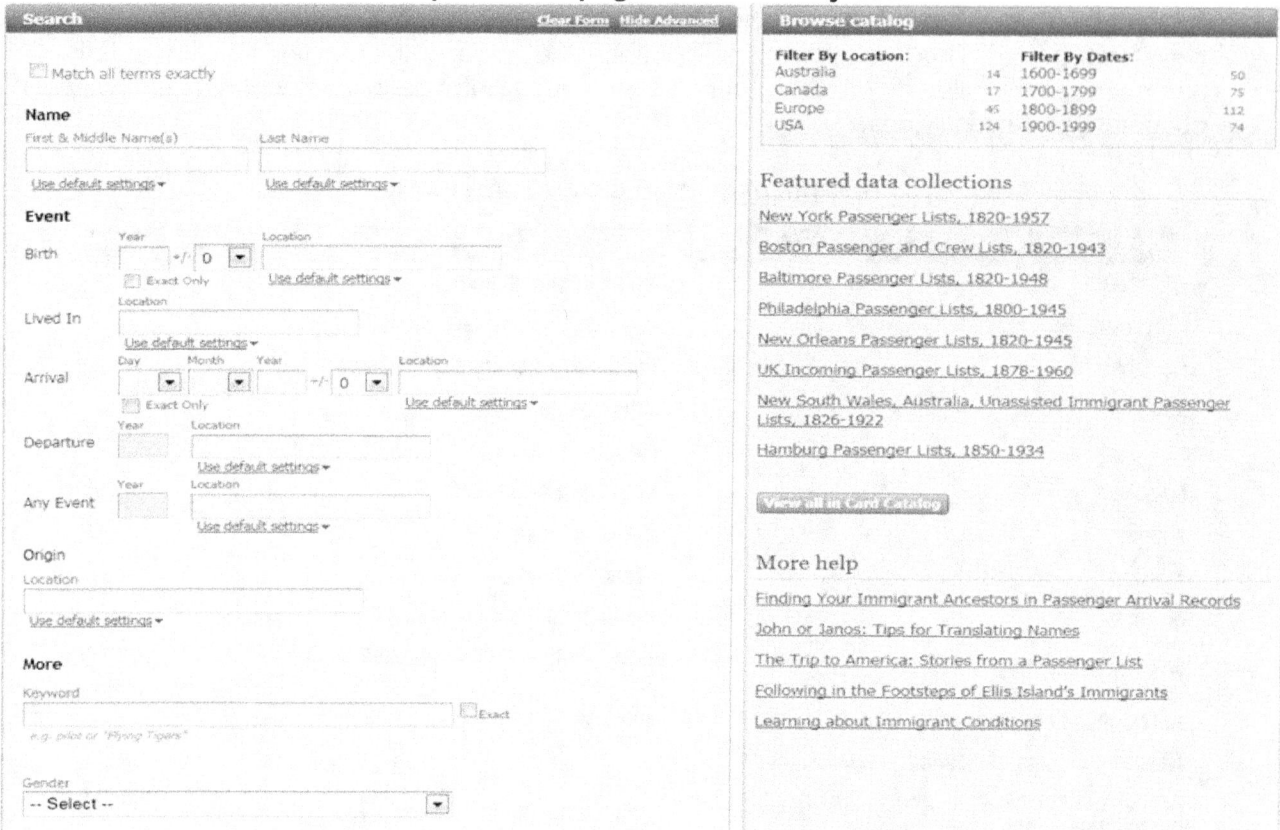

5. National Archives (all ports)

Paper copies of original passenger manifests from 1820 to 1959 can be obtained from the National Archives at their website http://www.archives.gov/ for $25. If you visit one of the Regional National Archive sites, you can obtain a paper copy for the nominal copying cost. Below is a sample page used to order passenger records from the website. Note that you need to register for a free account before you can sign onto this order screen.

Sample Passenger Manifest Order Page at the National Archives website

Order Information · Ship Passenger Arrival Records

[Save & Finish Later] [Cancel Order]

Do not use your browser's Back or Forward buttons while you are ordering.

Please provide the following information, if known. The * indicates this information is required to process your order.

Do you need to stop, do more research, and come back later? Then, use the **Save & Finish Later** button.

Not sure what something means or where to find the required information? Then, visit our Frequently Asked Questions section for more information.

* State of Entry:

* Port of Entry:

* Year of Arrival:

[Save & Finish Later] [Cancel Order]

Naturalization Petitions

The original naturalization act was passed in 1790 and stipulated that anyone who wanted to become a citizen of the United States must be a free white person who "behaved as a man of good moral character".

The steps to citizenship included:
1. Residence in the United States for at least two years
2. Residence in the state where they were applying for at least one year
3. Two witnesses must attest to the person's moral character and residency

Congress passed another Naturalization Act in 1795 that extended the residency requirement from two years to five years. The petitions were filed in county, territorial, state or federal courts. Knowing which court that was available is an important clue as to where to look for your ancestor's petition.

The Naturalization Petition is another document that describes the arrival of your ancestors and their early life in their new country. However, remember that naturalization was considered a privilege and not a requirement. The primary motivation for naturalization was the right to vote. Many immigrants did not go through the naturalization process. Some immigrants arrived with the intention of earning enough money to go back to their home country and buy land. Some of these ended up staying in the U.S. and never returning home. Census records can be used to determine if the immigrant was naturalized. 1890 was the first year individuals were asked if they were naturalized. On the census records, AL was listed for non-naturalized immigrants, PA was listed if they had submitted their declaration of intention and NA was listed if they have been naturalized.

Over the years, naturalization laws changed numerous times, but generally speaking the process required a Declaration of Intention and a Petition to be filed to become a citizen. Naturalization forms prior to 1906 included country of original, date of naturalization and the court where they were naturalized and usually did not include where they born or any other genealogical information.

Petitions submitted prior to 1906 did not require a town name. The pre-1906 petition usually listed only the country of birth.

Pre 1906 Naturalization Index card

67

Pre-1906 Naturalization Petition

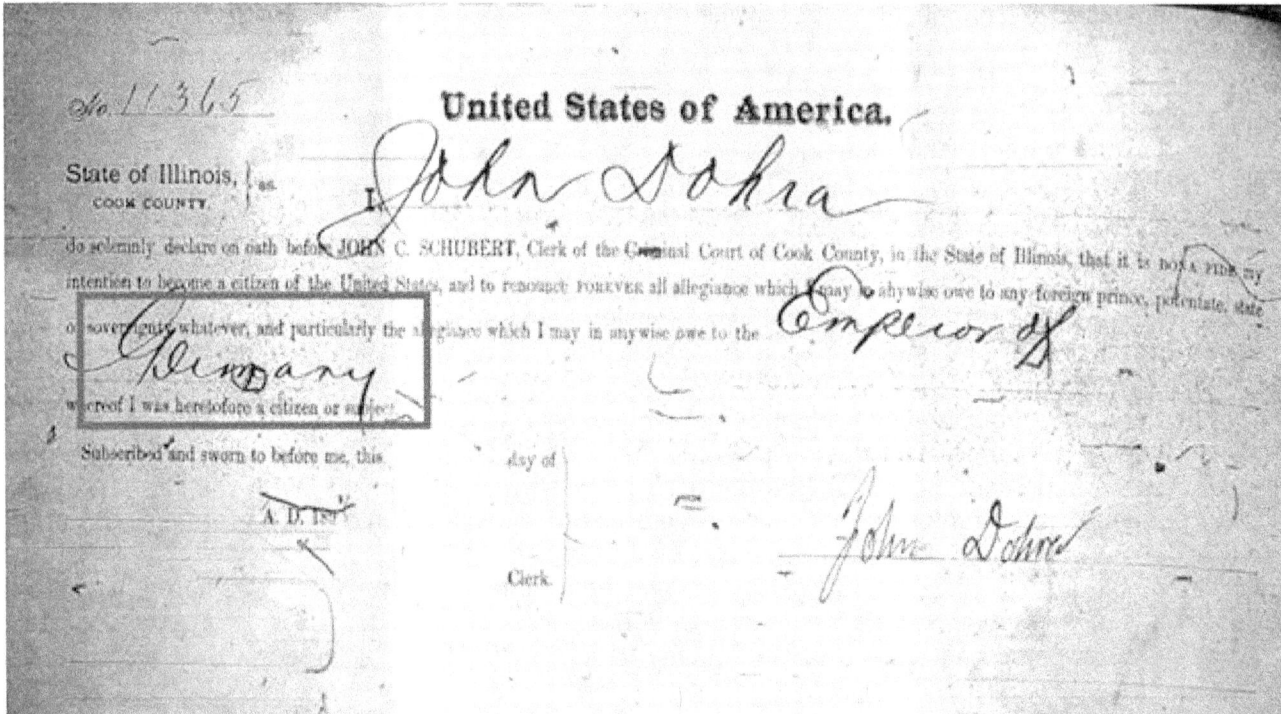

Petitions after 1906

Naturalization petitions submitted after 1906 listed many more details than previous years. New details that were listed included the applicant's birth date, birthplace, date of arrival, place of arrival and the name of the ship. If the immigrant was married, the petition also listed this information for their spouse and any children at the time of the petition. The new naturalization process also included a certificate of arrival for the applicant which listed the details of their arrival such as date of arrival, port and the name of the ship.

The birthplace listed on the petition could be the actual birthplace but it may also be where your ancestor was baptized. Either name will be an accurate name to direct you to where to look for the records of your ancestor in the "old country". Note that there may still be variations in how the name is written if the immigrant was not literate and the person filling out the form wrote the name phonetically. You will still need to find more names that will indicate what area the birthplace is located but you will have a very accurate piece to your puzzle.

The next illustration is the upper portion of the 1919 naturalization petition for my great-grandfather Martin Szabados. It lists that Martin was born on June 15, 1870 in Pankota, Hungary. He left Fiume and arrived in New York on January 10, 1907 on the ship Carpathia. The petition also listed the birthdates and birthplace for his wife Josephine and four of their children.

1919 Naturalization petition for Martin Szabados

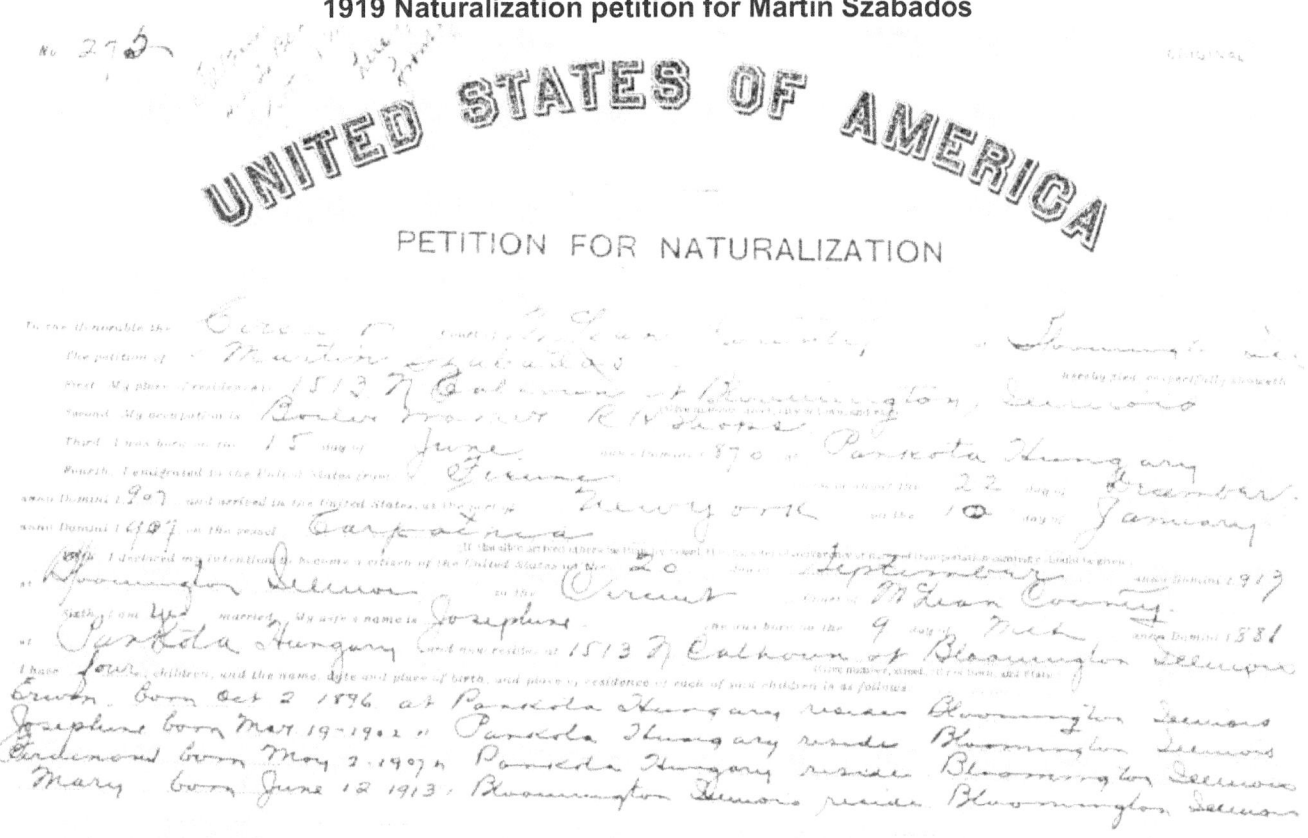

Below is the naturalization petition for my grandmother. It lists her birthplace as Andrejowo, Poland. There are a number of towns in Poland with this name so this entry only serves as one clue and other names are needed to find the exact location.

Naturalization Petitions after 1906

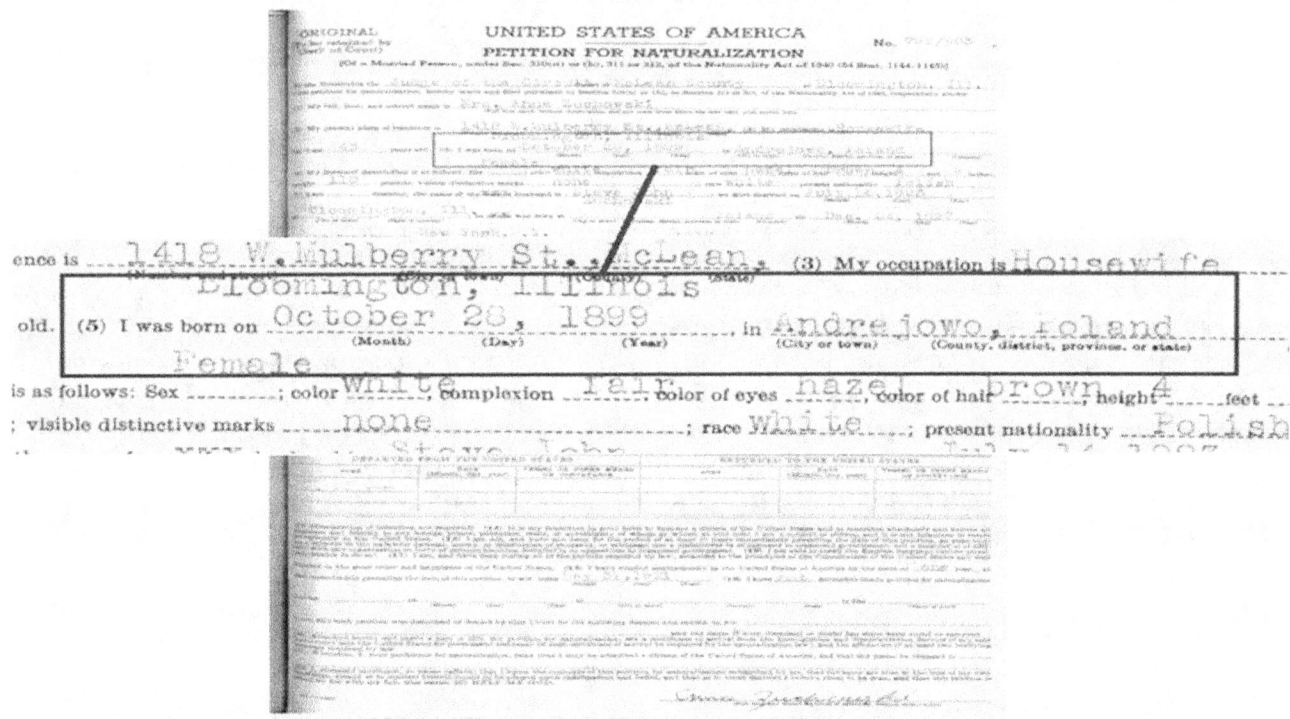

Where to obtain Naturalization petitions

Before requesting a copy of the naturalization petition, you should try to confirm that your ancestor was naturalized. The federal census records for 1900, 1910, 1920, 1930 and 1940 have a column that asks status of citizenship. Start by reviewing the 1940 census and then work back through the years until the census record indicates that your ancestor was not naturalized. This will give an estimate that they were naturalized between the two census years. If your ancestor did not become a citizen, search for naturalization papers for children and other relatives who were born in the "old country".

Other sources that may indicate if your ancestor became a citizen are naturalization indexes on ancestry.com and various county websites.

Below is a copy of the Naturalization Index card that I downloaded from Ancestry.com for my grandmother. Note that it lists that she was naturalized in the Circuit Court of McLean County in Bloomington, Illinois.

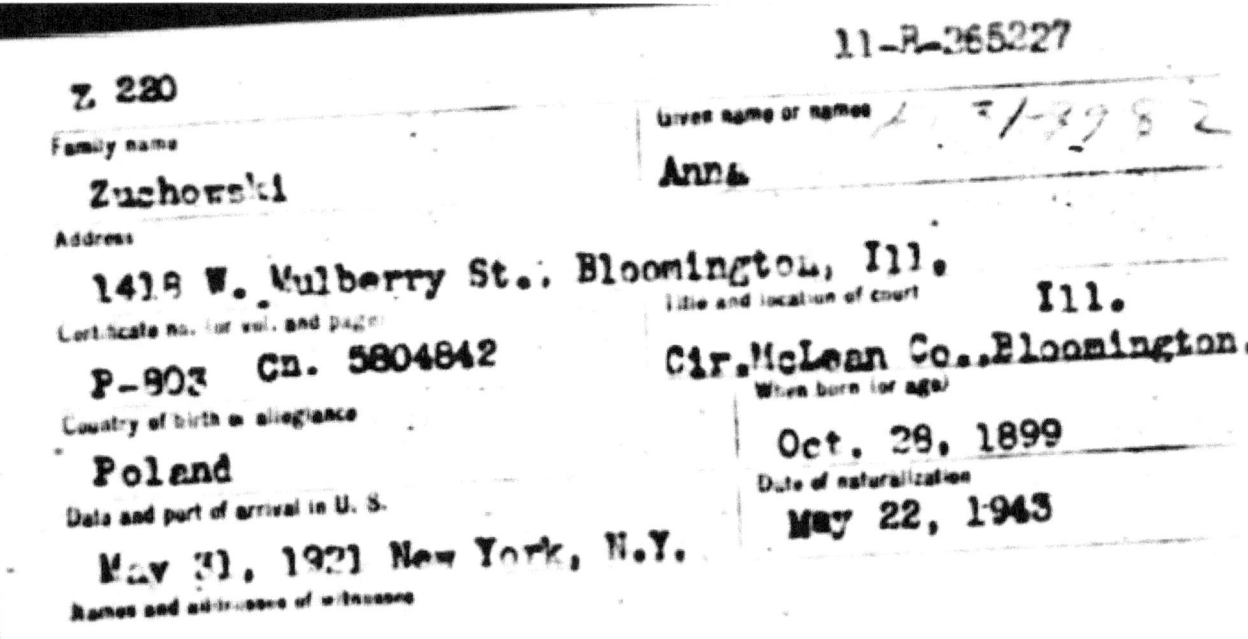

I also found my grandmother's naturalization information listed on the McLean County, Illinois website. Below is the information for my grandmother that is listed on Mclean County's Immigration page. Note that it is an extraction of information from her naturalization petition that is on file in the court records. Volunteers from the McLean County Genealogy Society extracted the information from these court files and compiled the database that is available on the McLean County website.

120 ZUCHOWSKI, ANNA Pet. for Nat. 803
Res. 1418 W. Mulberry St., Bloomington, Ill.; Housewife; b. 28 Oct. 1899 Andrejowo, Poland; Husband Steve John Zuchowski; mar. 14 July 1923 Bloomington, Ill.; he b. Poland 24 Dec. 1897; 2 children: John b. 18 Jan. 1927 Bloomington; Regina b. 19 May 1924 Bloomington; To US from Liverpool, Eng. to NY under name of Anna Chmielewski 31 May 1921 vessel unknown; Witnesses: Paul F. Jabsen, Heating Contractor; Martha Zulz, housewife; Oath of Allegiance 22 May 1943; Cert. Nat. 5804842

The next illustration is the home page for the Mclean County offices. Note the box where I point out where to select the immigration information page on the McLean County website.

Although you may find the naturalization index card on Ancestry.com or extracted naturalization information on a county website, you should always obtain a copy of the actual document. Sometimes errors are made when extracting the information and the letters of written information may be interpreted incorrectly and names are misspelled.

The Stark County Ohio website goes further and offers you the ability to download the actual documents. Below is the Naturalization petition for my great-grandmother Elizabeth Kovacs that I downloaded from their website.

Note that I have highlighted her birthplace as Kigjos, Bekes, Hungary and this was all the information that I needed to find her birth record.

ORIGINAL
(To be retained by
Clerk of Court)

UNITED STATES OF AMERICA

Vob. 79 P-251

No. 17651

PETITION FOR NATURALIZATION

[Of a Married Person, under Sec. 310(a) or (b), 311 or 312, of the Nationality Act of 1940 (54 Stat. 1144-1145)]

To the Honorable the .... **COMMON PLEAS** .... Court of .. **SUMMIT COUNTY** ...... at .... **AKRON, OHIO**
This petition for naturalization, hereby made and filed pursuant to Section 310(a) or (b), or Section 311 or 312, of the Nationality Act of 1940, respectfully shows:

(1) My full, true, and correct name is **ELIZABETH KOVACS**

(2) My present place of residence is **208 E. Voris St., Akron, Summit, Ohio** (3) My occupation is ...... **housewife**

(4) I am ... **62** .... years old. (5) I was born on .... **Oct. 29, 1878** .... in **Kigjos, Bekos, Hungary**

(6) My personal description is as follows: Sex **female**, color **white**, complexion **med.**, color of eyes **blue**, color of hair **br.**, height **4** feet **11** inches,
weight **164** pounds, visible distinctive marks **none**, race **Magyar**, present nationality **Hungary**

(7) I am .. **now**, married; the name of my husband is ... **Joseph** .... we were married on ... **June 29, 1929**

at .. **Akron, Ohio** .... he or she was born at .. **Szakaly, Hungary** ... on .. **Mar. 17, 1881**

entered the United States at .. **New York, NY** .... on .. **Sept. 29, 1912** for permanent residence in the United States, and now resides at

... **with me** .... and was naturalized on .. **Mar. 27, 1927** .... at .... **Akron, Ohio**

certificate No. .. **2150791** .... or became a citizen by
(7a) (If petition is filed under Section 311, Nationality Act of 1940) I have resided in the United States in marital union with my United States citizen spouse for at least 1 year immediately preceding the date of filing this petition for naturalization.
(7b) (If petition is filed under Section 312, Nationality Act of 1940) My husband or wife is a citizen of the United States, is in the employment of the Government of the United States, or of an American institution of research recognized as such by the Attorney General of the United States, or an American firm or corporation engaged in whole or in part in the development of foreign trade and commerce of the United States, or a subsidiary thereof, and such husband or wife is regularly stationed abroad in such employment. I intend in good faith to take up residence within the United States immediately upon the termination of such employment abroad.

(8) I have .. **two** .... children; and the name, sex, date and place of birth, and present place of residence of each of said children who is living, are as follows:
.... (f) **Elizabeth, born May 12, 1898 at Arad, Hungary, now res. Bloomington, Ill.**
.... (m) **George,** " **Sept. 21, 1904** " " **Akron, Ohio**

(9) My last place of foreign residence was .... **Pankota, Arad, Hungary** (10) I emigrated to the United States from .. **Fiume, Italy**

.... (11) My lawful entry for permanent residence in the United States was at .... **New York, NY** .... under the name

of **Takacs, Erssebet** .... on .. **June 29, 1910** ... on the **SS Carpathia** as shown by the certificate of my
arrival attached to this petition.

(12) Since my lawful entry for permanent residence, I have been .. **not** ... been absent from the United States, for a period or periods of 6 months or longer, as follows:

DEPARTED FROM THE UNITED STATES			RETURNED TO THE UNITED STATES		
PORT	DATE (Month, day, year)	VESSEL OR OTHER MEANS OF CONVEYANCE	PORT	DATE (Month, day, year)	VESSEL OR OTHER MEANS OF CONVEYANCE
none					

(13) (Declaration of intention not required) (14) It is my intention in good faith to become a citizen of the United States and to renounce absolutely and forever all allegiance and fidelity to any foreign prince, potentate, state, or sovereignty of whom or which at this time I am a subject or citizen, and it is my intention to reside permanently in the United States. (15) I am not, and have not been for the period of at least 10 years immediately preceding the date of this petition, an anarchist; nor a believer in the unlawful damage, injury, or destruction of property, or sabotage; nor a disbeliever in or opposed to organized government; nor a member of or affiliated with any organization or body of persons teaching disbelief in or opposition to organized government. (16) I am able to speak the English language (unless physically unable to do so). (17) I am, and have been during all the periods required by law, attached to the principles of the Constitution of the United States and well disposed to the good order and happiness of the United States. (18) I have resided continuously in the United States of America for the term of .. **3** .... years at least immediately preceding the date of this petition, to wit: since .... **June 29, 1910** .... (19) I have .. **not** .... heretofore made petition for naturalization

number .... on .... at .... in the
.... Court, and such petition was dismissed or denied by that Court for the following reasons and causes, to wit: ....
.... and the cause of such dismissal or denial has since been cured or removed.
(20) Attached hereto and made a part of this, my petition for naturalization, are a certificate of arrival from the Immigration and Naturalization Service of my said lawful entry into the United States for permanent residence (if such certificate of arrival is required by the naturalization law), and the affidavits of at least two verifying witnesses required by law.
(21) Wherefore, I, your petitioner for naturalization, pray that I may be admitted a citizen of the United States of America, and that my name be changed to ....

(22) I, aforesaid petitioner, do swear (affirm) that I know the contents of this petition for naturalization subscribed by me, that the same are true to the best of my own knowledge, except as to matters therein stated to be alleged upon information and belief, and that as to those matters I believe them to be true, and that this petition is signed by me with my full, true name: SO HELP ME GOD.

X Elizabeth Kovacs

Naturalization papers generated prior to 1906 should be held by the local courts where the immigrants were naturalized. After 1906, the courts were instructed to forward all naturalization papers to federal authorities and should now be held by the National Archives. However I have found some post 1906 naturalization papers that were still being held by county authorities. I would recommend requesting naturalization papers for your ancestors first from the National archives and if they can not supply you with a copy, you should then request the papers from the county court clerk where your ancestor lived. Some counties have indexed these records on line where you can search to see if the records for your ancestor are available from the county.

Below is the home page for the US National Archives (http://www.archives.gov/) and you will start the process to order naturalization petitions by selecting the "Shop Online" box. On the next page you want to select the "Request and Order Reproductions" box.

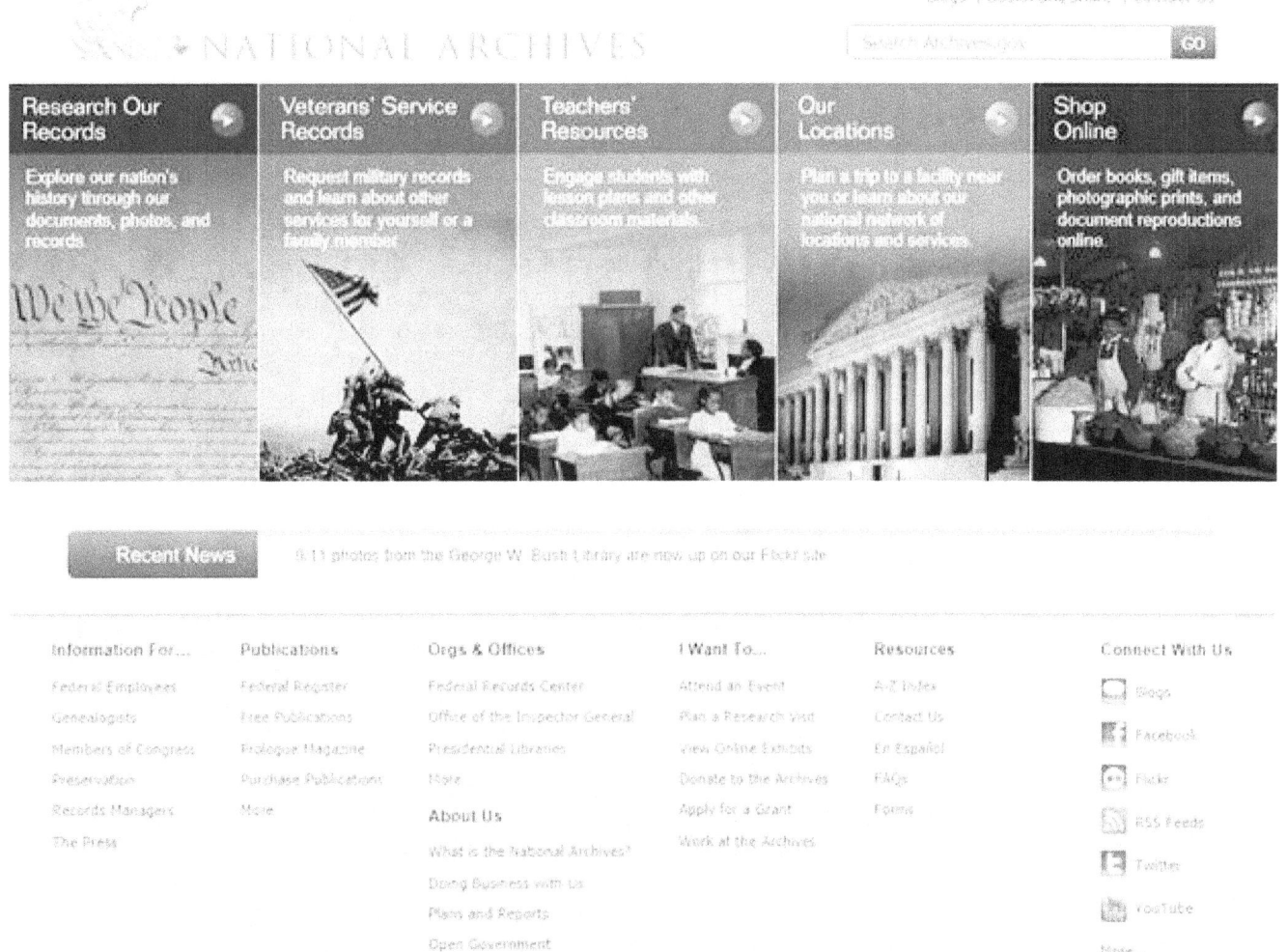

Continue going through 2-3 more pages until you are asked to fill out an online form with your ancestor's information.

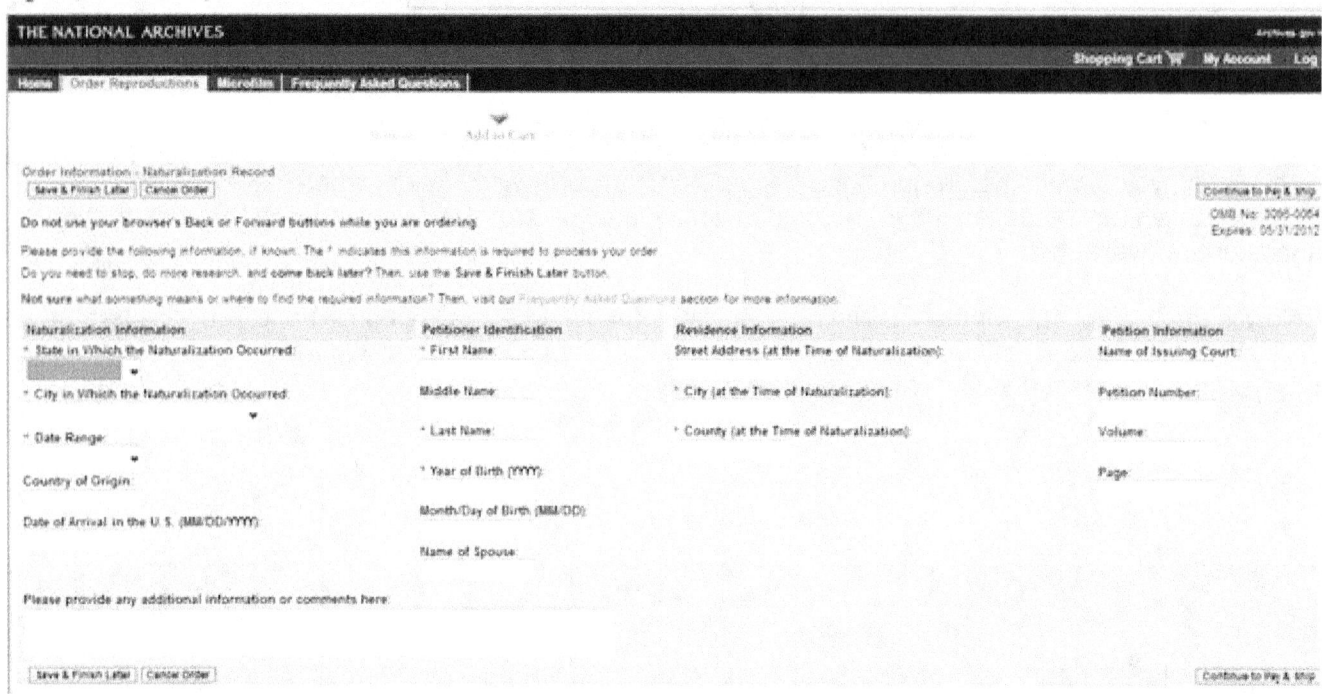

The researchers at the National Archives will respond to your request within 1-2 weeks. If they find the requested documents they will mail it to you and charge your credit card. If they do not find the documents they will give you some suggestions on where you can look next.

Note that many naturalization records can not be found. Using the above form to request a search by the National Archives would be a good place to start but you may have to contact the local county courts if the National Archives could not find them.

Other immigration documents - Exit Visas

In the late 1800s in many European countries, men had to obtain permission to leave their villages and emigrate. When requesting a passport, they had to submit several documents including a copy of the birth record, marriage, evidence of residence and occupation, supporting documents, and references. Applicants had to sign that they would waive their residence right to live in the village. If not, the village could be held liable for paying for return costs if emigration was refused or the people came back for other reasons.

The age and status of the man was one reason why emigration could be refused. Men had to prove that their military service obligation had been completed before they could leave. Sometimes this meant serving the required years or paying for someone else to take their place.

Also note that these legal documents were required by the passenger lines before passage could be sold to the immigrant. These legal documents would make it impossible for the name of the immigrant to be changed by the passenger line clerk or the immigration clerk in America.

The only source that I have found for Exit Visas of our immigrant ancestors are the desk drawers and shoe boxes filled with old documents and pictures found when our ancestors die.

1876 Exit Visa for Wenzel (James) Sirovatka

IM NAMEN SEINER KAISERL. UND KÖNIGL. APOSTOLISCHEN MAJESTÄT

FRANZ JOSEPH I.

KAISERS VON ÖSTERREICH,

KÖNIGS VON BÖHMEN U. S. W. UND APOSTOLISCHEN KÖNIGS VON UNGARN

REISE-PASS

für *Sirovatka Wenzel*

Geburtsjahr *1846*

Statur *mittel*

Gesicht *länglich*

Haare *braun*

Augen *lichtblau*

Mund *regulär*

Nase *groß & gebogen*

Besondere Kennzeichen:

Charakter Beschäftigung *Jäger Cöfzdar*

wohnhaft zu *Groß-Roebrova*

im Bezirke *Moldautein*

Kreis (Comitat) *Bradweis*

Kronland *Böhmen*

Eigenhändige Unterschrift: *Vaslav Sirovatka*

Dieselbe reiset

von

der k. k. öster

Monarchie

nach den Deutsch

Staaten

Dieser Pass ist gültig auf

Sechs Monate

Moldautein am *30 ten März 1876.*

Im Namen Sr. Excellenz des k. k. Herrn Statthalters:

Der k. k. Bezirkshauptmann

Summary for Immigragration Documentation
1. Passenger manifests will document your ancestors arrival in the United States.
2. The format of the passenger manifest changed over the years and information listed may include the immigrant's last residence, which they left, and the address and who was at their final destination and their birthplace.
3. Passenger manifest information can be found at the National Archives (regional locations and online), some local libraries, Ancestry.com, Ellis Island website and Castle Gardens website
4. Copies of the actual manifest can be obtained from Ancestry.com, Ellis Island website, National Archives (online and regional locations) and some local libraries
5. Naturalization petitions submitted after 1906 will have a birthplace listed.
6. Check the Clerk of the County where ancestors lived to see if they list information for Naturalization petitions or their availability.
7. If the County website does not offer naturalization petitions, use National Archive website to request petitions.
8. Exit Visas are a wealth of accurate information but are rare and are only found if the immigrants were careful to save them.

8 FINDING MORE RECORDS

In this chapter we will discuss military, land/court and employment records which are three more types of records that may add genealogical information to your family history. We waited to discuss these categories of records because they are much harder to find but if the records are found they can add some very rich facts about your ancestors.

Military Records Overview

Examples of some of the useful military records that I found are World I and World War II draft registrations which list the date of birth and birthplace of the applicants. Other useful sources that may be available are Civil War and Revolutionary War pension documents which list the date, place of birth and many additional facts such as the name of their spouse and children, the unit they serve with in the war and some describe the actions that they fought in. I have tried to list the military records that are available in the following pages. This chapter will first discuss the availability military service records and then records that are available for each of the military conflicts from the Korean War going back to the Revolutionary War.

Military Service Records

To get information and forms to request military service records, use the Veterans Service Record tab on the home page on the National Archives website (http://www.archives.gov/). If available, the military service file for your ancestor should contain many interesting genealogical facts. Service records for personnel who served after 1914 are stored at the National Personnel Records Center in St Louis, Missouri. However, many Army records from WW I or WW II were destroyed in a 1973 fire. National Archives personnel are attempting to replace some of the information lost in this fire by reconstructing individual files for Army personnel from documents that were stored in files at other locations. This requires searching all military files that were not in the St Louis Records Center at the time of the file and trying to find documents that pertain to individuals and then placing copies of these documents in new files for the individuals. This will not replace all of the facts contained in the files that were burned but hopefully they will capture some facts of the service of personnel that were affected by the fire.

Navy records were not burned in the fire and are available.

After initially being told the files of my father and grandfather were destroyed, I was able to obtain copies of parts of the files for my father (WW II) and grandfather (WW I) through a request to my congresswoman. The copies that I received were those recovered by the National Archives personnel and were stored at the National Archives. To obtain the copies from the National Archives, I had to pay a $60 fee to the St Louis Records Center to cover the cost of the copies.

The illustration shown to the right is the WW I enlistment paper for my grandfather. I was able to obtain about 20 pages from the archives by asking my congresswoman's for help. The writing on this page is faded but it lists a Chicago address and the name of his sister Mary Lapinski. It also lists that he was born in Russia but the name of the town is faded. Notice the black edges that were damaged and probably recovered from the fire.

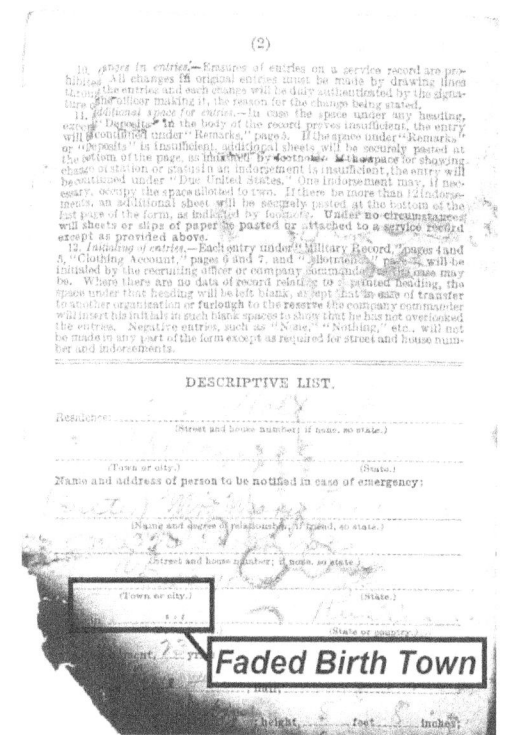

The page in my grandfather's enlistment papers that listed his place of birth

Compiled Military Service Records (CMSR)

The service records for men who served in volunteer units during conflicts before 1914 were put in files that were called Compiled Military Service Records (CMSR). These records were for soldiers and officers and were filed by regiment. If a soldier served in more than one regiment, he will have a CMSR in the files for each regiment that he served. The CMSRs included biographical and medical information, physical description, pay vouchers, marital status, leave requests and commendations. An index of CMSRs is available on the NARA website.

Regular Army Enlistment Papers 1798-1894 and Register of Enlistments in the Regular Army 1798-1914

The files for regular army soldiers can be found in the Regular Army Enlistment Papers 1798-1894 and the Register of Enlistments in the Regular Army 1798-1914 files. The papers found in these files will show the date and the place of enlistment, age, place of birth, occupation, physical description and information about the soldier's company and regiment.

Regular Army Officers

Personnel files were not kept for U.S. Army officers until 1863. However, information on officers prior to 1863 can be found in a series of files that contain letters received by the Adjutant General's office. There are three files:

- Letters received by the Office of the Adjutant General, 1805-1821
- Letters received by the Office of the Adjutant General, 1822-1860
- Letters received by the Office of the Adjutant General, 1861-1870

You can also view the microfilm at the NARA in Washington, DC.

The book *Historical Register and Dictionary of the United Sates Army, from its Organization, September 29, 1789 to March 2*, 1903 by Francis B Heitman is an excellent source of information on Army officers. It provides a brief history of each officer and a list of battles and actions in which the U.S. Army fought. The 1069 page book can be viewed online at Google Books.

Early Navy and Marine Records

The enlistment papers for Navy personnel were called Rendezvous Reports. This was the name for the station where men could enlist into the navy. The information was sent to the Navy Department and included place of residence, date and term of enlistment, occupation and physical description. Similar records were kept for marine personnel.

To obtain the Navy or Marine records you must contact the NARA directly by using the instructions found on its form NATF 86. Does not use form NATF 86 to obtain information for Navy or Marine Records. Contact the NARA online at www.archives.gov/contact

or by writing to:
Archives 1 Reference (NWCT1F-Military)
Textual Archives Services Division
National Archives and Records Administration
700 Pennsylvania Avenue NW
Washington, DC 20408-0001

Summary of Military Records from Each War
Korean War

The Korean War was fought from June 25, 1950 to July 27, 1953. The United States and other members of the United Nations came to the aid of South Korea and eventually fought both Chinese and North Korean forces. The armistice agreement that was signed restored the border between the Koreas near the 38th Parallel and created the Korean Demilitarized Zone (DMZ), a 2.5-mile (4.0 km) wide buffer zone between the two Koreas.

Ancestry.com has six databases that list military records for the Korean War. These include indexes that list U.S. prisoners of war, casualties, New York residents who were naturalized and Alabama soldiers who fought in the Korean War.

Note that there are two databases that list prisoners and two that list casualties. Search all four databases for your ancestor because they may not overlap records completely. All four are indexes of extracted information and do not show the actual documents. The information for these databases was extracted from original documents at the National Archives at College Park, College Park, Maryland and the Korean War Listing from the American Battle Monuments Commission.

The New York Naturalization Index lists extracted information for veterans New York Southern District who were naturalized in Korea while serving in the military. The information on the index cards were extracted from the naturalization petitions that were obtained from the NARA' Northeast Region Archives. The Ancestry.com database provides only an image of the index card and you will need to request a copy of the complete petition through the NARA website as discussed in chapter six.

Beginning in 1862, congress passed a series of acts that were designed to encourage aliens to enlist in the military. Their enlistment did not grant automatic citizenship but sped up the process based on their honorable service. The required waiting period between the declaration and filing the petition was waived if the alien received an honorable discharge.

The Korean War database for Alabama Soldiers was created by the staff members from the Alabama Department of Archives and History (ADAH) Staffers extracted details from various newspaper articles, brochures, reference correspondence, photocopies and typescripts of original documents to document the military service of persons for Alabama during the Korean War. The index cards can include details such as name, branch of the military served in, rank, residence/address, event dates (wounded, missing in action, rotation returnee, etc.), sources, source dates, and names of family members/next of kin. Cards may also include some military personnel from the time period who were not necessarily deployed to Korea.

World War II and World War I
Because many of the records for World War I and World War II army personnel were lost in the 1973 fire, I found the World War I and World War II draft registrations as the easiest military records to obtain for these wars. They usually list place of birth, their address, the name of a contact person and their employer. The World War II draft registration was called the "Old Man's Draft Registration" because it required men who were born on or after April 28, 1877 and on or before February 16, 1897 to register.

One format of the World War I draft registration also is useful. Three formats of World War I draft registration cards were used and the last format used listed town of birth but the first two did not. All three also listed a person who would always know how to contact the registrant. This person usually listed the person's wife but for unmarried men, it usually listed the name of one of their parents. The form also listed their address, occupation and employer.

Ancestry.com, Familysearch.org and Fold3.com offer databases that contain the WW I and WW II draft registration cards. Familysearch.org also offers an index that lists the WW I soldiers who were naturalized.

The next two illustrations are examples of the World War I and World War II draft registrations that list some useful information of ancestor's birthplaces. Also remember that the WW I draft registrations used three different formats and only the last one listed place of birth. The town names given on these two documents should be accurate because it was given by the person who was born there. Again use these names as clues to help locate the area and note that the town name that is given may be a misspelling.

WW I draft registration

WW II draft registration

REGISTRATION CARD—(Men born on or after April 28, 1877 and on or before February 16, 1897)

SERIAL NUMBER	1 NAME (Print)		ORDER NUMBER
U 1542	John ... Chmielski		

2. PLACE OF RESIDENCE (Print)

45 Ash St., Jersey City ... Hudson ... N.J.

(Number and street) (Town, township, village or city) (County) (State)

[THE PLACE OF RESIDENCE GIVEN ON THE LINE ABOVE WILL DETERMINE LOCAL BOARD JURISDICTION; LINE 2 OF REGISTRATION CERTIFICATE WILL BE IDENTICAL]

3. MAILING ADDRESS

Same

[Mailing address if other than place indicated on line 2. If same insert word same]

4. TELEPHONE	5. AGE IN YEARS	6. PLACE OF BIRTH
None	47	Czuluw
(Exchange) (Number)	DATE OF BIRTH 12 - 24 - 1894 (Mo.) (Day) (Yr.)	(Town or county) Poland (State or country)

7 NAME AND ADDRESS OF PERSON WHO WILL ALWAYS KNOW YOUR ADDRESS

Mrs. Stella Chmielewski - 45 Ash St.

8. EMPLOYER'S NAME AND ADDRESS

Lehigh Valley Railroad

9. PLACE OF EMPLOYMENT OR BUSINESS

Washington St. , Jersey City , Hudson, N.J.

(Number and street or R.F.D. number) (Town) (County) (State)

I AFFIRM THAT I HAVE VERIFIED ABOVE ANSWERS AND THAT THEY ARE TRUE.

John Chmielewski

(Registrant's signature)

D.S.S. Form 1
(Revised 4-1-42)   (over)   16—21630-3

1898 to 1902 - Boxer Rebellion, Spanish American War and the Philippine Insurrection

From 1898 to 1902, American military forces were engaged in three conflicts in foreign lands - the Boxer Rebellion in China, the Spanish-American War in Cuba and the Philippine Islands and the Philippine Insurrections in the Philippine Islands.

Ancestry.com and Familysearch.org have a number of records in their online databases that you can use to check to see if your ancestor served in the Spanish-American War, Boxer Rebellion or the Philippine Insurrection.

Ancestry.com has databases that list the names of volunteers and service men from the states of Connecticut, Indiana, Massachusetts, Michigan, Minnesota and Oregon.

Familysearch.org also has a number of databases that may cover veterans of Spanish-American War, Boxer Rebellion or the Philippine Insurrection:
- United States, Veterans Administration Pension Payment Cards, 1907-1933
- United States, Remarried Widows Index to Pension Applications, 1887-1942
- United States, Registers of Enlistments in the U. S. Army, 1798 - 1914
- United States, Old War Pension Index, 1815-1926
- United States, Navy Widows' Certificates, 1861-1910
- United States, Index to Service Records, War with Spain, 1898
- United States, Index to General Correspondence of the Pension Office, 1889-1904
- United States, General Index to Pension Files, 1861-1934
- United States, National Homes for Disabled Volunteer Soldiers, 1866-1938
- United States, Applications for Headstones for Military Veterans, 1925-1941 (Civil War or later)

Civil War 1861 to 1865

The American Civil War began on April 12, 1861 and lasted four years. It is interesting from a genealogical viewpoint because some people may find ancestors who fought for the Union and others who fought for the Confederate forces. Also, researchers will find that more records are available from the Civil War than other U.S. conflicts.

Below is the Civil War discharge paper for Silas Howard. This document was past down through four generations and is an example of the importance of documents like this. It was very important in the his family history because it is one of the few documents that have been found that lists when and where he was born.

Besides family oral history, family letters, personal journals and civil war personal items, there are many sources for Civil War information.
- Genealogy websites such as Ancestry.com, Ancestry Library Edition, Familysearch.org, Fold3.com and newspaper databanks
- U.S. National Archives
- Park Service Archives

Online sources should be searched first to find basic information about your ancestors. The websites offer many indexes listing such as date of enlistment, place of enlistment and military unit. Some documents are also available for these sources. Most data is available for Union soldiers but there are also many Confederate records available from confederate states records. One other online source is Wikipedia which has unit histories and battlefield histories that will help you know when and where your ancestor was during the Civil War.

Visits to the National Archives, State Archives and National Park Service Battle sites will yield many more documents about your ancestors but of course you will need the specific information you find on the online sources before you know what and where to search.
- When you are at the battlefield sites ask the historian who is on site for any information about your ancestor and his unit. They normally need some time to retrieve the files but once they have delivered them two you you should be able to find many details of the battle that refer to your ancestor or his unit that go beyond what you find in the history books.
- Since many Civil War military units were volunteer groups, their state archives will contain many files of enlistments, muster rolls and pensions.
- The National Archives in Washington, D.C. contains the service files for each folder, the records and papers of each military unit and pension records. Copies of these files will be available in the appropriate regional NARA sites but will be on film and may not be copies of all the pages found in the actual file. Another hint to gain access to the full files is to obtain researcher status instead of a family member.

Indian Wars
American Indian Wars is the name used in the United States to describe a series of conflicts between the native peoples of North America and the American settlers or the federal government. This includes conflicts during the colonial period until sometime in 1922 with the end of the last Apache uprising. The wars resulted from the arrival of European colonizers who continuously sought to expand their territory, pushing the indigenous populations westwards.

There are fewer military records for soldiers who fought in these conflicts than in other conflicts. Search for indexes of colonial militias, rosters of U.S. soldiers prior to WW I and U.S. military pension records on Familysearch.org and Ancestry.com.

War of 1812
The War of 1812 was fought between the forces of the United States and those of the British Empire. The Americans declared war in 1812 for several reasons which included trade restrictions due to Britain's ongoing war with France, the impressments of American merchant sailors into the Royal Navy, British support of American Indian tribes against American expansion and possible American desire to annex Canada.

Records for veterans of the War of 1812 that are offered by Ancestry.com include the Bounty Land warrants, military service records, pension records, muster rolls, prisoners of war and many state records. Familysearch.org offers pension files and services records for veterans of the War of 1812.

Revolutionary War

When the Revolutionary War began, the 13 colonies lacked a professional army or navy. Each colony sponsored local militia. Militiamen were lightly armed, had little training, and usually did not have uniforms. Their units served for only a few weeks or months at a time, were reluctant to travel far from home and thus were unavailable for extended operations, and lacked the training and discipline of soldiers with more experience. Seeking to coordinate military efforts, the Continental Congress established (on paper) a regular army on June 14, 1775, and appointed George Washington as commander-in-chief. The development of the Continental Army was always a work in progress, and Washington used both his regulars and state militia throughout the war.

Ancestry.com, Fold3.com, Worldvitalrecords.com, HeritageQuest and Familysearch.org have numerous databases that can be searched for your ancestors service during the Revolutionary War.

- HeritageQuest usually can be found on your local library's databases and one section set of records offered by HeritageQuest are the Revolutionary War pension applications. The application usually list descriptions of the battles they fought in, their birthplace and their birth date. Sometimes it also lists the names of their wife and children.
- Fold3.com offers the Revolutionary War Service Records.
- Fold3.com and FamilySearch offers an index of the *United States, Revolutionary War Compiled Service Records, 1775-1783.* Ancestry.com offers images of the register pages that contain these records but they do not have to allow you to search by name. I would recommend that you use the indexes on either familysearch.org or Fold3.com to find your ancestor and then use the document source info that is listed in the index to find the pages in the ancestry.com database.
- Pensions and bounty land warrants were issued to compensate Revolutionary War veterans for their service and can be found on Ancestry.com and Familysearch.org.
- Ancestry.com and Familysearch.org have indexes of soldiers who fought as part of the many state militias and lists of the Loyalists who fought with the British forces.
- Worldvitalrecords.com offers numerous databases for Revolutionary War veterans. Some of the databases are the same as the other websites but some are different.

Summary for Military Records

1. Many WW I and WWII U.S. Army records were destroyed in a 1973 fire and are not available.
2. Family oral history may give you hints that a family served in these conflicts and hopefully the databases listed above will help you verify this fact.
3. Most of these databases are indexes, so it is important to note the source of the extracted information and seek out the original documents.
4. Also remember to revisit the various websites because new databases are being added to their online collections regularly.
5. Worldvitalrecords.com offers numerous military databases. Some of the databases are the same as the other websites but some are different and this fact makes this website attractive to search occasionally. It is a paid subscription website but offers a 7 day free trail and a monthly subscription option.

County Records

Many county records from both the county offices and the courtroom can yield valuable family history. Birth, marriage and death were recorded by county officials and many naturalization papers were filed in the county courts. These records were discussed in chapter five and six. In this chapter we will discuss the genealogical information that you may find in land records and probate records. Other court records that could list your ancestors are civil trials, criminal trials and jury rosters but we will not discuss in detail in this book.

Land records

There are usually two land or deed records for each place your ancestor owned. One was when they purchased the property and the other was when they sold it. Some counties may keep all transactions for the property on one ledger so the ownership of the property can be tracked while it is in existence. These records are found in the county recorder's office. Tax records will also be available will be available in the county assessor's office. These documents will help you find the location of each property that your ancestor owned and will give you valuable information about their history such as the price they paid for the property, any improvements that affected the taxes, when was the property built and how much your ancestor received when the sold the property.

Another important document that would be useful in your genealogical research would be a tract map for the county. This normally indicates the owner of each section of land and should show you're the location of your ancestors land if they were a farmer. Historical tract maps may be available from the local county historical society and possibly at the recorder's office.

Portion of the 1892 Plat of Swan River Township, Morrison County, Minnesota - note that each section is labeled with the name of the owner

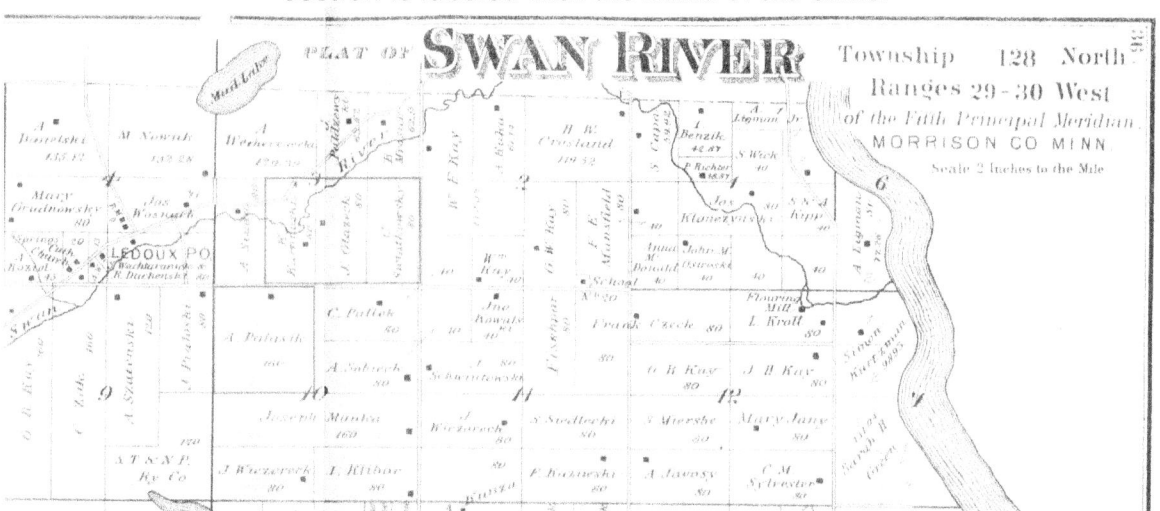

The Homestead Act

The Homestead Act was signed into law by President Abraham Lincoln on May 20, 1862 and allowed a person to apply for ownership of typically 160 acres of of undeveloped federal land west of the Mississippi River land. The law required three steps: file an application, improve the land, and file for a deed or title. The applicant had to be 21 or older or be the head of a family, had lived on the land for five years and show evidence of having made improvements.

The Enlarged Homestead Act was passed in 1909 to increase the number acres to 320 for lands that were not prime farmland along rivers but could only use dryland farming methods.

Forty percent of the applicants (over 1.6 million homesteads) who started the process completed the process and were granted title to their homestead claim. The title was recorded by the county recorder and copies of the land patent that was granted can be found on the website for the Bureau of Land

Management (www.blm.gov). This covered more than 420,000 square miles. This accounts for about 10% of the land of the United United States.

Below is a sample of the Land Patent was granted.

Pierre 011159   4—1023-R.

The United States of America,

To all to whom these presents shall come, Greeting:

WHEREAS, a Certificate of the Register of the Land Office at **Pierre, South Dakota,** has been deposited in the General Land Office, whereby it appears that full payment has been made by the claimant

Elmer Howard

according to the provisions of the Act of Congress of April 24, 1820, entitled "An Act making further provision for the sale of the Public Lands" and the acts supplemental thereto, for the **northeast quarter of Section twenty-nine in Township four north of Range twenty-two east of the Black Hills Meridian, South Dakota, containing one hundred sixty acres,**

according to the Official Plat of the Survey of the said Land, returned to the GENERAL LAND OFFICE by the Surveyor-General:

NOW KNOW YE, That the UNITED STATES OF AMERICA, in consideration of the premises, and in conformity with the several Acts of Congress in such case made and provided, HAS GIVEN AND GRANTED, and by these presents DOES GIVE AND GRANT, unto the said claimant and to the heirs of the said claimant the Tract above described; TO HAVE AND TO HOLD the same, together with all the rights, privileges, immunities, and appurtenances, of whatsoever nature, thereunto belonging, unto the said claimant and to the heirs and assigns of the said claimant forever; subject to any vested and accrued water rights for mining, agricultural, manufacturing, or other purposes, and rights to ditches and reservoirs used in connection with such water rights, as may be recognized and acknowledged by the local customs, laws, and decisions of courts; and there is reserved from the lands hereby granted, a right of way thereon for ditches or canals constructed by the authority of the United States.

IN TESTIMONY WHEREOF, I,   **Woodrow Wilson**

President of the United States of America, have caused these letters to be made Patent, and the Seal of the General Land Office to be hereunto affixed.

GIVEN under my hand, at the City of Washington, the   FOURTEENTH

(SEAL)   day of   AUGUST   in the year of our Lord one thousand

nine hundred and   THIRTEEN   and of the Independence of the

United States the one hundred and   THIRTY-EIGHTH.

By the President: *Woodrow Wilson*

By   *M. O. LeRoy* Secretary,

L. Q. C. Lamar

Recorder of the General Land Office.

RECORD OF PATENTS: Patent Number   **350254**
6—2171

Probate records

Probate records are court records dealing with the distribution of a person's estate after death. They were recorded much earlier n history than birth, marriage, and death registration. Probate records are very useful for family history research because they recorded the death date, names of heirs, family members, guardians, relationships, residences and inventories of the estate. Also remember that probate records were not created for every person who died.

The next illustration is an example of an affidavit that was used to probate the estate of a farmer and transfer his property to his wife. The Affidavit was given by two of the sons of a deceased farmer.

1908 General Affidavit given by two sons of the deceased about the death

Summary of Legal Records
1. The names listed on legal documents may be of additional relatives or friends of the family. Researching files for their records may yield more information about your ancestor.
2. The addresses listed on the documents will point you to the properties they owned or where they lived. This may give you clues about their lives and also give you opportunities to take pictures of the properties where they lived.
3. Other legal documents such as probate files and wills may give you an inventory of their property and the names of more family members.

Employment/Retirement Records

Due to privacy issues, employment records for your ancestor will be difficult to obtain from their employer. They will probably acknowledge the years that your ancestor was employed but refuse to release any individual information. This is unfortunate because the employment application will have many personal facts of your ancestor such as birthdates, birthplace, education and previous employment.

What employment records are available?

Retirement papers for all railroad employees

I have found that the retirement files for railroad employees are available from the Railroad Retirement Board (RRB). Legislation was enacted in 1934, 1935, and 1937 to establish a railroad retirement system. RRB administers the pensions of all railroad employees from all companies and their records are separate from the social security program that was legislated in 1935. Their files include not only the employee's pension applications but also numerous papers concerning service dates and in some case the amount of pay. Marriage and insurance information may also be included.

For more information on requesting genealogical information from the Railroad Retirement Board go to their Genealogy Research web page at: http://www.rrb.gov/mep/genealogy.asp. Your request and payment of $27 fee will give you copies of all papers in their files. Allow about 30-60 days for the RRB to find the files and send you copies.

Below is a copy of a page from my grandfather's railroad retirement file that lists his birthplace.

More Railroad Employment Records

If your ancestor worked for the railroad but did not receive a pension, the Railroad Retirement Board will not have any file on them. You will need to search historical archives to find these records if they exist.

Pullman-Standard was the leading producer of railroad passenger cars in the early 1900s. The company also played a leading role as an arsenal during WW I and WW II when it produced freight cars, tanks, and munitions for America's war efforts during both World Wars. Thousands of employees from Northwest Indiana and Chicago contributed to the success of Pullman-Standard at their Hammond,

Michigan City, and Chicago locations. Since employees routinely transferred within the Pullman-Standard plants located in Indiana and Illinois, information on a particular employee may be scattered between sources in Indiana and in Illinois

I found that the South Suburban Genealogical Society (SSGS) in Crestwood, Illinois was able to save the personnel files for the employees from the now closed Pullman Standard Car Works plant in Chicago, Illinois. In 1982, the Society somehow was able to save employment files that cover the period from about 1900 through World War II and account for approximately 152,000 Pullman employees. Prior to South Suburban taking possession of the records, they had been stored in a wood kiln in Hammond, Indiana. In January of 1983, the SSGS started alphabetizing more than a million Pullman employment documents (they were previously kept in numerical order). It took six years and 2,560 volunteer hours to clean, re-box, and index this massive collection. The files may also include many personal papers such as birth certificates. The Pullman collection is not open to the public. Research is done only by authorized volunteers. SSGS staff will search the Pullman files at no charge to find if your ancestor is in the records but there is a fee if you order a copy of the file. The efforts of the South Suburban Genealogical Society are just one example of what files may be available.

The Calumet Regional Archives holds the employee records for the Pullman Car Works that were in Hammond, Indiana. These records have been cataloged by volunteers from the Northwest Indiana Genealogical Society and the index can be searched on the NWIGS website using their Online Archives and/or Research Resources page.   http://www.rootsweb.ancestry.com/~innwigs/
More Pullman employee records can be found at the Newberry Library in Chicago which has the files for the Pullman car service employees (such as Porters, etc).

Many railroad historical societies have been able to save railroad employment records. The Chicago and Northwestern Historical Society have many employee records that contain great genealogy information. Unfortunately, many other records were destroyed as railroads merged or went out of business. Some records were also destroyed just because they were old and the railroad did not see any value in keeping records for dead people. To find these records you will have to know for which railroad your ancestor worked. A useful source for this information is books called "The Official Railroad Guide." These books were published every 3 months and listed the schedule for every train in all towns in the United States. It also contained an index that listed all towns in alphabetical order that had a train station. To find which railroad company your ancestor worked for, find one of these guides for the appropriate time period and look for the town where your ancestor lived. Next, the page for the town will name of the railroad that serviced the town. Your should be able to find a copy of the Official Railroad Guide at most railroad historical groups, some state libraries, some university libraries and large genealogy libraries.

Employment records for other companies
More employment records from defunct companies may have been saved by local genealogy or historical groups. As an example, I found the employee cards from the Gary Screw and Bolt Company listed on the NWIGS web site. Most records for defunct companies were destroyed when their offices were cleared out. However, try contacting local societies where your ancestor worked to see if they have any employment records for local companies - you may find a treasure. Note, this is not true for companies that were merged or purchased since the files of the old company would have been merged into the new company.

Social Security Records
Social Security Applications are another employment record that may be obtained. The Social Security Act was signed into law by Franklin D. Roosevelt in 1935 to provide retirement income to workers in their old age. Employees were required to register for a Social Security card and number. This process required proof of their birthdates and the application will list not only their birthdates but also their place of birth, the names of their parents, the residence, their occupation and their employer.

Records that may be available from Social Security for your ancestors include the Application for a Social Security card (form SS-5) and information from the claims folder for past recipients of benefits. To obtain any of this information from Social Security you will need to file a Freedom of Information Act request and Form SSA-711. You can also use the form letter shown in the next illustration instead of Form SSA-711. The letter should list the name and social security number of your ancestor. Note that recent concerns about privacy issues have brought proposals to remove the Social Security Death Index from public viewing. Recent requests have been fulfilled with the names of the parents removed unless proof of their death accompanies the request.

The next illustration shows the Ancestry.com results page for a search of the SS Death index. Note the highlighted box to the left for ordering the original application. Using this will generate the letter with all information filled in.

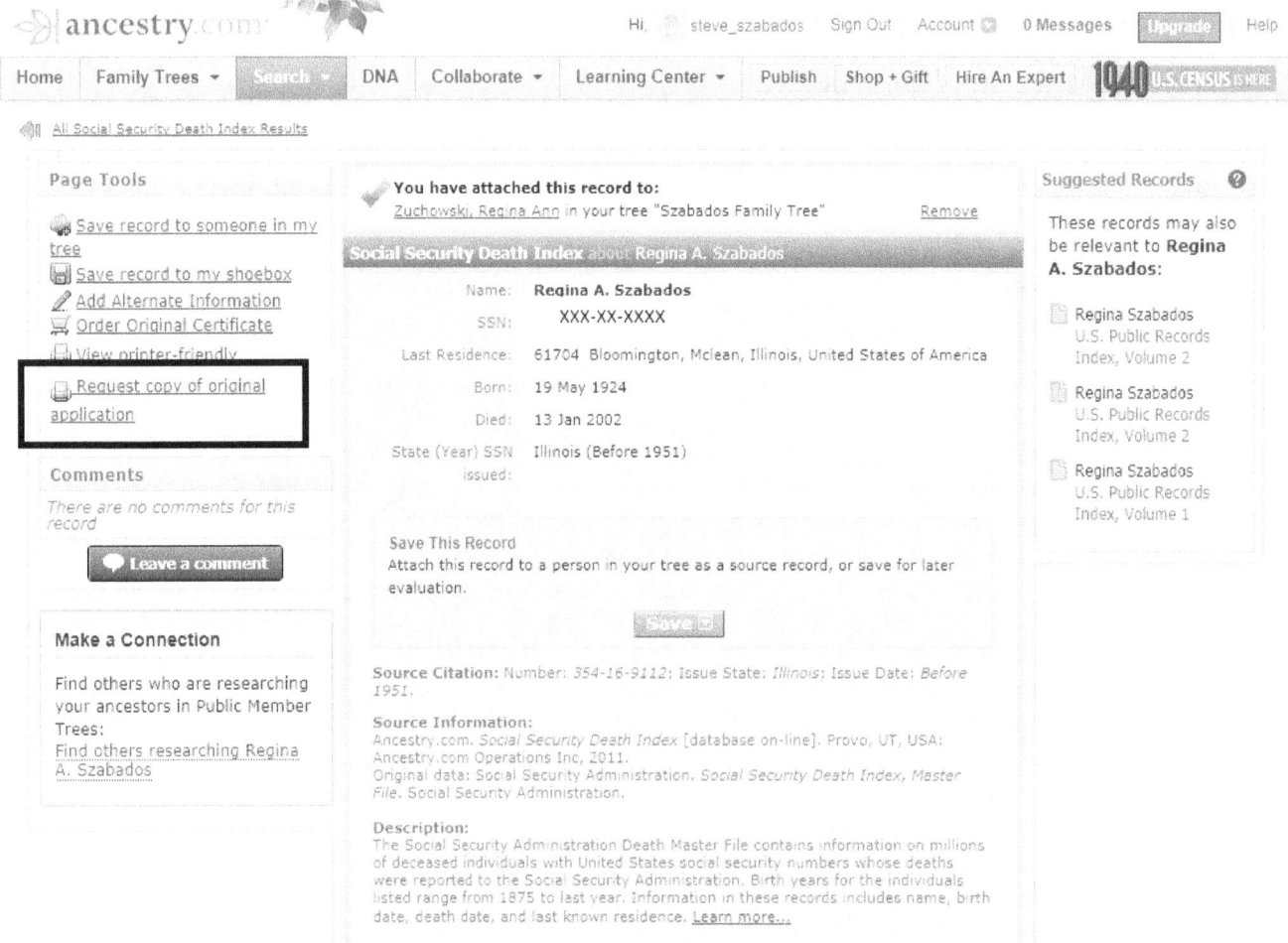

Without an SSN, you will need to supply the person's full name, date and place of birth, and parents' full names to locate the record. Social Security did not begin keeping records until 1936; therefore, they do not have records about people who died before then. Privacy concerns may change past procedures and proof of death may be requested before the Social Security Administration will process your request.

The fee for searching Social Security records for the form SS-5 is $27 when the SSN is known and $29 when the number is unknown or is incorrect. They accept checks, money orders VISA, MasterCard, Discover, American Express or Diners Club. Include the appropriate credit card number, along with the expiration date of the credit card with your written request. Checks or money orders should be made payable to the Social Security Administration.

Form SSA-711 can be downloaded from the Social Security Administration website and used to request a copy of your ancestors application for a Social Security Number but is not required. You can also send a letter to the administration with the needed information. Next illustration is a form letter that you can use to request a copy of the application.

If their Social Security card was not saved in their papers you may be able to find their Social Security number by finding their death in the Social Security Death index which is available on Ancestry.com and familysearch.org

Letter Requesting SS Application

Social Security Administration
OEO FOIA Workgroup
300 N. Green Street
P.O. Box 33022
Baltimore, Maryland 21290-3022

Please send me a photocopy of the actual SS-5 application for a Social Security card filed by the person listed below.

I obtained this information from the Social Security Death Master file at Ancestry.com, Inc. who obtained it from the Social Security Death Master file, originally compiled by the Social Security Administration.

My understanding is that the fee is $27, when the Social Security number is provided or $29 if the Social Security number is unknown or incorrect. Enclosed is a check or money order for $_____, made payable to the Social Security Administration.

Name of Person
Social Security Number
Birth Date
Death Date

Thank you for your assistance.

Sincerely,

Your Name
Your Address
Your Daytime Phone Number

A copy of the claim file may also be available and the cost to search for a claim file is $14 when you provide the SSN. You may be charged 10 cents a page for copies. Please note that claim files are usually destroyed within a few years of the final decision on the claim, so they will not have claim files for most people. Requests for claim files should be sent to:

Social Security Administration
Freedom of Information Officer
6401 Security Boulevard
Baltimore, MD 21235-0001

Note: Recent concerns with identity theft and privacy have led to stricter policies of supplying a copy of social security applications. They cannot release information on living persons without their written consent. Parents are assumed alive unless proof of death accompanies the request. This may thwart the purpose of your request because you may be seeking a copy of the application to find the names of the parents. Hopefully, current efforts to tight restrictions on these requests will be soften to allow the release of the names of the parents if the assumed ages are beyond most life spans.

The next illustration shows the Social Security application of my grandfather. Note that his birthplace was written phonetically (Czyvef instead of Czyzew).

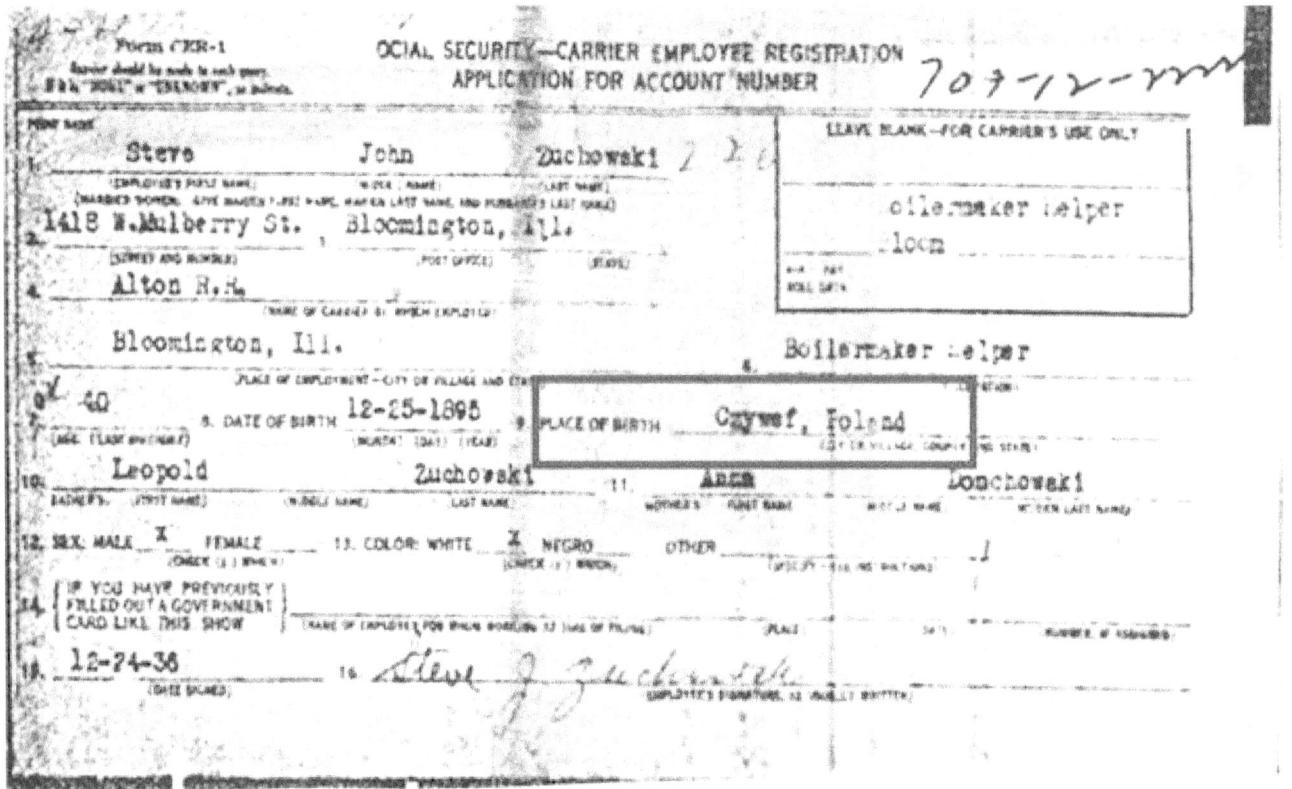

Summary for Employment Records

1. Most employments records may not be available due to privacy concerns and due to the fact that older files would be stored in archives and not available for public viewing.
2. The Railroad Retirement Board does offer copies of the files for their retirees for a search fee.
3. Also some genealogy societies and libraries have been able to save the personnel files for some defunct companies and these would be available for genealogical research.
4. The application process for a Social Security number required a document showing the date of birth for the applicant and the application also included a space for place of birth that was shown on the document of birth. You can request a copy of the application by using the form letter provided by the Social Security Administration and paying $27 or $29.

Genealogy Societies

Many local genealogy societies have worked hard to build collections of documents and information that pertain to the counties where they live. They were generally formed to find, preserve and share the genealogical information for their area. Their files are excellent sources for hard to find birth, marriage and death records, family bibles, family histories, county histories, cemetery records, obituaries and many more. Most societies have websites that list their collections and contact information. Some of your questions for them may be answered by email or phone but if you list is long you should plan to visit their archive for help.

Revisit your Sources

It is important to continue to revisit your source - especially online databases. As your research progresses you will finding more facts about your ancestors and internet databases are regularly adding records to their online files. Some of the new records added to the online databases may be for your ancestors or their siblings. By adding your new facts to the search criteria you may be able to find results that did not show up in previous searches.

Usually I use only the family surname when I return to search previous databases. One example of my success using this technique led to the names of brothers and sisters of one ancestor. I then researched the marriage records for these siblings and I was able to identify their birthplace in Poland. When I searched the Polish records, I was able to extend the family back three more generations.

Another example was when I found a 1935 biography of the brother of an ancestor. This had been added to an online family tree in the previous year. The biography included references to the name of the Catholic Church the family attended and when I called the church, I found the marriage record for the ancestor. This record listed where the bride and groom were baptized in Poland and I was again able to extend the family back three more generations.

These are only a few examples where I eventually was able to find information to breakdown some of my brickwalls.

9 TIPS FOR SEARCHING ONLINE DATABASES

The development of the internet for sources of genealogy records has helped the genealogist be more efficient in their research efforts. Many documents can be found online. Using online indexes can also be helpful and time efficient because the index will help the researcher know where to go to get a copy of the document and give a time period to search the actual files.

Websites such as Ancestry.com and Familysearch.org that have multiple databases may be difficult to search because they have such a large amount of information available. Their home pages offer a chance to do a general search of all of their databases at one time. This search does not allow you to enter enough criteria to narrow your search and this type of search may produce too many results that do not pertain to your ancestor. However, when I search on one database I usually find my records faster. An example of this is when I search the federal census records, I will search the records for only one year such as 1930. The individual databases allow me to enter more criteria and this usually produces more results that pertain to the person that I am seeking on the first page of the results. I also initially use criteria that I know are accurate. Using information that may be inaccurate may give too many results that do not pertain to my ancestor. The phrase "Quality over quantity" does apply in research efforts.

More search tips
Next there are three methods to find difficult records.
1. Wildcards
2. First names and other criteria but not last names
3. Soundex

Using Wildcards
Spelling variations in names will cause some records for your ancestors to hide from your viewing. The use of wildcards with portions of their names may help you to find these records. Wildcards are characters that can stand in for any letter of a name to catch alternate spellings or mis-spellings of the name. On most websites, an asterisk * stands in for zero or more letters in a name, and a question mark? stands in for exactly one letter.

An example of the use of "?"
- The use of "anders?n" will yield both Anderson and Andersen

An example of "*"
- The use of "D*borwski" will yield Dabrowski, Dombrowski and Dambrowski

To use wildcards effectively, you must first understand the language that databases use. Often in genealogy work you come across the names of individuals that are not a match for the person you are looking for but are very similar but will give us too many results to search efficiently. Many times a wildcard can be used to filter out the results that keep popping up that we're not interested in. Using this method, wildcards will eliminate hundreds of records to review and potentially save many hours of research time.

To use wildcards on websites, you should learn the rules for their use on each website. The rules for the use of wildcards on Ancestry.com and Familysearch.org seem to be the same. At least three non-wildcard characters must be in a name. You can use a wildcard as the first or last letter, but not both. You can also use the wildcard in the middle of the name.

The EllisIsland.org database doesn't return results for wildcard searches but their advanced search options allow for some flexibility with partial names. The next illustration shows the options available for the options available in the First Name dropdown menu. Similar choices are available with the dropdown menus for Last Name, Year of Birth, Year of Arrival, Name of Town and Name of Passenger Ship.

ADVANCED PASSENGER SEARCH (1892 - 1924 ARRIVALS)

Please Note: The "Sounds Like" search requires a minimum of 1 character for the first name and 5 characters for the last name.

Use Advanced Search to specify additional details for a passenger arriving through Ellis Island from 1892-1924. You do not need to use every field shown below, but can provide any combination of information you may have.

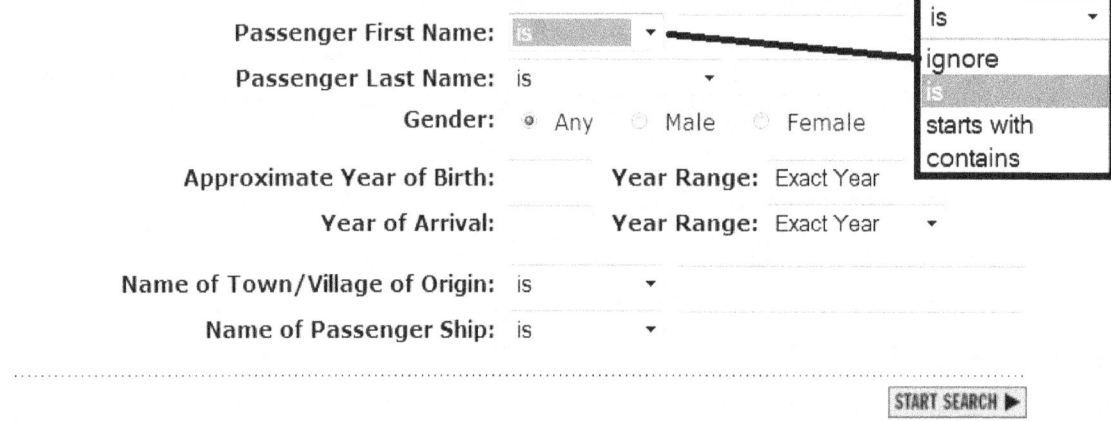

Search technique when surnames have been changed or mis-spelled horribly

As we discussed early, some families changed their surname because their name was mis-spelled or mis-pronounced most of the time. I have found that finding these families becomes easier if you search using only their first names and other criteria. An example of this is my search for the Jubert family that changed their name from Dziubek.

When I first started searching for the Jubert family records, I found only the 1910 census record, the 1920 census record and the the WW I draft registration for their son Joseph. The draft registration listed that Joseph was born on February 26, 1894 in Ironwood, Michigan (see the first illustration on the following pages). When I searched for the birth record for Joseph Jubert, I did not find it. I then searched again entering only Joseph, his year of birth, the first name of his father and the first name of his mother. I found a record for Joe Gubak that listed the correct date and parents. I then used the same method to search for the birth records for the rest of the children and found them listed with the surnames of Duback, Juback and Jubak. I also used the same method to find the marriage of the parents. In the 1900 census, the family was listed under the name of Sulek. The third and fourth illustrations show that the list of names for Sulek family matches the list of names for the Jubert family on the 1910 census. The death certificates for the parents did use the correct name of Dziubek but the sons continued to use Jubert as their surname. One baptismal certificate for one of the grandsons listed his father's surname as Jubert but the priest also listed Dziubek in parentheses on the certificate.

WW I Draft Registration for Joseph Jubert

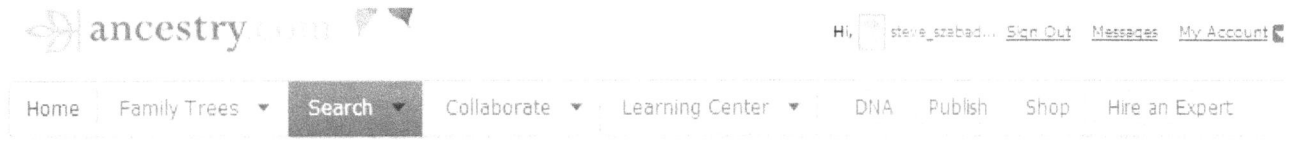

Search Results for Joseph, born in 1894 in Michigan with parents John and Maria.

ancestry Hi, steve_szabad... Sign Out   Messages   My Account

| Home | Family Trees ▼ | Search ▼ | Collaborate ▼ | Learning Center ▼ | DNA | Publish | Shop | Hire an Expert |

Ranked Search Results - 1900 United States Federal Census

You searched for **Joseph** born in **Michigan** Refine your search

All Census & Voter Lists Results   Show All matches ▼   Viewing **1-50** Next »

View Record	Name	Parent or Spouse Names	Home in 1900 (City,County,State)	Birth Date	Birthplace	Race	Relation	View Image
View Record	Joseph Sulek	John, Maria	Chicago Ward 15, Cook, Illinois	Feb 1894	Michigan	White	Son	🔍
View Record	Joseph Duratep	John, Maria	Chicago Ward 10, Cook, Illinois	Oct 1895	Illinois	White	Son	🔍
View Record	Joseph L Farley	John, Maria	Chicago Ward 9, Cook, Illinois	Apr 1893	Illinois	White	Son	🔍
View Record	Joseph E Harmon	John, Maria	Chicago Ward 10, Cook, Illinois	Oct 1893	Illinois	White	Son	🔍
View Record	Joseph Janousek	John, Maria	Chicago Ward 10, Cook, Illinois	Nov 1894	Illinois	White	Son	🔍
View Record	Joseph Mcdonald	John, Maria	Chicago Ward 31, Cook, Illinois	Oct 1892	Illinois	White	Son	🔍

The Sulek Family listed on the 1900 Census record

Sulek, John	Head	W	m	Dec 1864	35	m	11			Poland (Ger)	
Maria	Wife	W	f	Feb 1872	28	m	11	6	4	Poland (Ger)
John	Son	W	m	Dec 1889	10	S				Michigan
Sophia	Daughter	W	f	Mar 1891	9	S				Michigan
Francis	Daughter	W	f	Mar 1893	7	S				Michigan
Joseph	Son	W	m	Feb 1894	6	S				Michigan
Ethie	Daughter	W	f	Mar 1898	2	S				Illinois
Marie	Daughter	W	f	Jan 1900	6/12	S				Illinois

The Jubert Family listed on the 1910 Census record

Jubert, Jan	Head	M	W	44	m	21			Ger	Polish
—, Mary	wife	F	W	39	m	21	2	8	Ger	Polish
—, Jan	son	M	W	20	S				Michigan
—, Sofie	daughter	F	W	19	S				Michigan
—, Frances	daughter	F	W	17	S				Michigan
—, Joe	son	M	W	16	S				Michigan
—, Hattie	daughter	F	W	11	S				Illinois
—, Mary	daughter	F	W	10	S				Illinois
—, Nell	daughter	F	W	7	S				Illinois
—, Helen	daughter	F	W	5	S				Illinois

You may not be able to find some census records and passenger manifests using the above advanced search methods. The first and last names of your ancestors may have been very difficult to read and the record was indexed using a very different set of names. In this case, browsing the individual pages may be needed to find your ancestor. In order to narrow your search and to minimize the number of pages you search try to find facts such as addresses from other sources.

For census records, determine the address where your ancestor lived at the time of the census by looking at their address listed on documents that recorded other events at about the same time of the census. These can be birth records, marriage records, death records and voter registrations. City directories are another good source of addresses. Once you have identified their address, you can determine the enumeration district that contained this address and reduce your search to about 20 to 50 pages.

To find passenger manifests, another source is the information listed on their naturalization petitions. To process their naturalization they had to obtain a certificate of arrival that listed the name of the ship and the date their arrival. If their naturalization petition is not found you can get a hint of when they arrived from the year of arrival listed on the 1900, 1910, 1920 and 1930 census records. However, you will still need more information to narrow the time range because searching all of the arrival records for a given year is a very large task.

Soundex Searches

The Soundex system is a phonetic algorithm for indexing names by sound, as pronounced in English. The goal is for similar sounding names to be found when their database is searched despite minor differences in spelling. The algorithm code will mainly use consonants. A vowel will be used in the code only if it is the first letter. Soundex is the most widely known of all phonetic algorithms in part because it is a standard feature of popular database software.

The Soundex system was developed by Robert C. Russell and Margaret K. Odell and patented in 1918 and 1922.[ ] A variation called American Soundex was used in the 1930s for an analysis of the US censuses records from 1890 through 1920. The National Archives and Records Administration (NARA) maintains the current rule set for the official implementation of Soundex used by the U.S. Government and are explained in the General Information Leaflet 55, "Using the Census Soundex".

Some online genealogy websites allowed entering soundex codes but most have incorporated a phonetic spelling option in their search engine algorithm. However searching the census records naturalization records at the National Archives will require use of the soundex system.

Every soundex code consists of a letter and three numbers. The letter is always the first letter of the surname. The numbers are assigned to the remaining letters of the surname according to the soundex rules that shown in the next two illustration. My name of Szabados has a soundex code of S-132.

S as the first letter of my name, the Z & A are ignored, B is coded as 1, the A is ignored, the D is coded as 2, the O is ignored and the S is dropped because the code already has 3 numbers.

SOUNDEX CODING GUIDE

Disregard the letters A, E, I, O, U, H, W and Y.

Number	Represents the Letters
1	B, F, P, V
2	C, G, J, K, Q, S, X, Z
3	D, T
4	L
5	M, N
6	R

Additional Soundex Coding Rules

1. Names with double letters - If the surname has any double letters, they should be treated as one letter.
   - For example - Gutierrez is coded as G-232 (G, 3 for T, 6 for the first R, ignore the second R, 2 for the Z)

2. Names with letters side-by-side that have the same soundex code number - If the surname has different letters side-by-side that have the same number in the soundex guide, they should be treated as one letter.

For example - Tymczak is coded as T-522 (T, 5 for the M, 2 for the C, irnore the Z, 2 for the K), since the vowel A separates the Z and the K, the K is coded.

3. Names with Prefixes - If a surname has a prefix, such as Van, Con, De, Di, La or Le, the code the name both with and without the prefixbecause the surname may be listed under either code. However mc and Mac are not considered prefixes.
    - For example - VanDeusen may be coded two ways
        V-532 (V, 5 for N, 3 for D 2 for S)
        D-250 (D, 2 for the S, 5 for the N, 0 added to give the code the third number)
4. Consonant Separators - If a vowel separates two consonants that have the same soundex code, the consonant to the right of the vowel is coded.
    - For example - Ashcraft is coded A-261 (A, 2 for the S, ignore the C, 6 for the R, 1 for the F), It is not coded A-226.

Summary for searching records

1. Begin your genealogy research with the internet databases due the the speed and efficient search methods that can be used.
2. Much of the information on the internet is in the form of indexes that will point you to well to find the documents but many document images are being added daily.
3. Use wildcards to overcome variations in the spelling of a name
4. Use only first names and other criteria to eliminate problems with the spelling of the surname.
5. Use non-census records to determine the enumeration district if you need to view individual pages to find your ancestors.
6. Many records such as census and passenger records are listed on more than one website. Search all of the websites until found. The information may have been indexed differently on the different websites and may be easier to find on one of them and not the others.
7. Be sure to search the files of local genealogy societies.
8. Check history books to see if borders changed and your ancestors may be in located in neighboring locations.
9. Revisit your resources when you find new information or to check if new information has been added to your resource. This may also help breakdown some of your brick walls.
10. Do not use internet sources exclusively. Learn where other documents are located to obtain copies of the actual document.
11. Last, but certainly not least, be sure to keep a Research Log while you are searching your various sources. Mark down who you searched for, where you searched for them, which variations you tried, and what your results were. This will help keep you from spinning your wheels and duplicating your research time as you move ahead with your research.

10 RESEARCH TRIPS

Using the internet is a great way to start your research but eventually you will have to plan a research trip to continue your research. The trip may be to a cemetery, the neighborhood where your ancestor lived, a local genealogy archive, a government archive or a government office. Your visit is needed to do your own hands on research because the amount of research is too large to be done by email, letter or phone.

You must prepare very carefully for this trip to be successful. This chapter will discuss a checklist of things you should do in this preparation.

Your first step would be to decide where you are going. Normally there are a number of places you will need to go to continue your research. Some may be close by and others may be many miles away. I suggest your first trip should be to the closest facility to where you live and which requires a simple list of research needs. This could be a cemetery, a local genealogy archives or just visiting the neighborhood where your ancestor lived. Your research needs could be to record tombstone inscriptions, searching for copies of obituaries or taking pictures of the homes where your ancestors lived. These close and simple trips will help you develop your organizational skills for longer and more complicated trips.

Avoid frustration and increase your research time by carefully planning your research trips:
- Determine what records are available at the location where the trip is planned
- Compile a list of specific documents to search for and list the people and their details for quick reference while searching.
- Call ahead to make sure the facility will be open at the time of your planned trip.
- Get organized and pack

1. Know What's Available
Before visiting a location you will need to determine what records or information are available. Visit their website to check what they have listed and also call to ask specific questions on the types of records that may list your ancestors. Another question is to determine what unique records they have that are not available any other place and decide how these documents may help your research. Browsing the documents and books that are unique to this facility may include manuscript collections, unpublished papers and records, photographs and local history books. It makes sense to try to use all the resources available at the location you are visiting and not miss any opportunities.

Another important part of your planning will be to make sure you are planning to visit the right location. Some county borders changed over time. You may find that your ancestors may have lived on one farm for all of their lives but their records may be stored in another than the current county due to past boundary changes.

2. Know What You Want
Once you know what information is available at the location, deciding what family or person to focus on is the next step of the planning process. Preparing your lists will make your trip more successful and minimize your frustration and aggravation. It is very important to have a research plan so that you stay focused. Your lists should include:
- specific facts you want to prove or disprove
- records you need to find on specific people
- what documents you want to browse to see if they mention your ancestors
- make a list of questions you need to ask at the location

Having a purpose in mind for your research trip will make your planning easier and will help keep you focused while on your trip. Just deciding to leave tomorrow to do genealogical research many miles away may sound tempting, but planning can help you make your trip a more efficient use of your time and money.

If your trip is a long distance from your home, double-check for alternate sources close to home. You should have already checked for FHC films that you could order, but large nearby university libraries may have collections that will give you the information that you were planning to get on your trip.

3. Make sure the location is open the day you plan to be there
Visit the website for the facility will give you useful information as to their hours and what collections they have. However, once you have decided on the time period you want to visit them, you need to call to verify that the facility will be open and the collections you want to research will be available. Another phone call done one to two weeks prior to the planned visit should also be made to make sure their schedule has not changed.

Examples of what could go wrong:
- When you arrive at the archive, you find they are open but renovations are being done and the records you want are on carts.
- You do not call and you try to visit the archive on the day when they are closed due to a local holiday.
- You visit the archive during a local festival and you are not be able to find a room at a local hotel
- You find that the library is open when you arrive but the genealogy room has more limited hours and you are delayed for a few days.

Every facility has times which are busier than others. Find out which days of the weeks have the lowest amount of visitors. Visiting on these days will allow you more time to ask questions of the staff, it will be easier for you to find a good parking spot, more open microfilm reader will be available and getting records from the stacks will take less time.

It is also very important that you know where you are going. During one of your phone calls you should ask if there are any special instructions to finding the facility. If this is in a remote area physical or online maps may not be accurate. Make sure you have road maps and directions.

4. Learn the Procedures of the Location
Before you arrive at the location, you will need to determine what restrictions there are on the use of the documents at the archive or library. Restrictions may affect your access to the records during your visit. At some facilities you may need to be member of a specific genealogical or historical society. Records at some large libraries may be stored at an offsite facility or vault that will require ordering the documents or film before arrival. Also some records may require that they be viewed in the presence of an archivist due to the age of the document.

You should also learn if there are restrictions on the use of cameras, laptops and portable scanners? Are the records available on microfilm or in there original form? Are pens allowed or are only pencils used? Is a wireless connection available? Is the availability of the records closed stack or open stack? Is there an online or card index available for the collection?

Obtaining copies are also very important. Are copy machines in open areas or are staff only allowed to copy documents? Can copies be made of all documents? What is the cost of the copies? Do microfilm readers connected to printers? Can flash drives be used to save copies?

If the facility is in a large city, ask if the location can be reach by public transportation. Is there nearby parking? Does the location have a cafeteria or lunchroom or nearby restaurants?

5. Get your Files and Tools Organized for the Trip

It is important to take the right stuff on your trip. As part of your planning it will be helpful to make lots of lists;

- People to research and the facts that you know about them
- Genealogy files
- Questions
- Maps, directions and contact information
- Tools allowed - laptop, scanner, pens, notebooks, coins etc
- Always remember to take a magnifying glass to help in reading old records.

While on your trip, it is important to be able to access your own family tree. Some people prefer to do this by bringing copies pages of pedigree charts, family group sheets, and notes. This information can be stored on a laptop but if laptops are not allowed in the facility organize your information in a ring binder and carry that on your trip.

Take only copies of documents with you and leave your original documents behind. No one will probably steal them, but forgetting them somewhere is a definite possibility.

Special note for cemetery visits

If you are you planning on taking photographs of tombstones or making tombstone rubbings on your trip, practice at a local cemetery. The time to learn is not at a cemetery many miles from home and on the last day of your trip with a storm approaching.

6. Other Packing for a Research Trip

Here are some items to pack for your trip that are not genealogy related.

- **Laptop computer**. If you have one, take it on your trip even if it is not allowed in the research facility. It is a great communication tool and Wifi connections are available at most hotels and coffee shops.
- **Cell Phone -** Never leave for a trip without your cell phone. Remember to take your charger with you.
- **GPS** – Very handy gadget to have on a trip. It is difficult to have a map for everyplace that you go and a GPS unit will help you find the way. Also, if you visit a cemetery, record the grave location on your GPS unit to help find your way back on a later visit.
- **Camera**. Even if cameras are not allowed in the research facility, use your camera to record your trip.
- **Suitable clothing**. Look at the weather forecast and be prepared for the worst.
- **Umbrella**. Again always be prepared for changes in the weather.
- **Snacks**. You will need extra energy.

7. Summary

- Visiting an area where your ancestors lived can be an extremely exciting and rewarding experience. Walking the land and visiting the cemeteries where they were buried will bring you closer to them than a piece of paper could ever do.
- It seems easy to jump in the car and go, but advance planning is an integral part of the process. It would be sad and a tremendous waste of your time and money to show up at a courthouse and find that it was closed due to a local holiday.
- You also need to know ahead of time what to pack for your trip. What genealogy tools are allowed in the facility and what files should you bring?
- Where are you going? What is the weather forecast?
- Another enjoyable aspect of the trip is talking to the archivists or genealogy volunteers.
- With a little preparation, your trip has more of a chance of running smoothly and efficiently.
- Start thinking about your next genealogy research trip.

11 MESSAGE BOARDS AND ONLINE FAMILY TREES

Use of Genealogy Message Boards

There are many great opportunities to share and exchange information on the internet. One method to do this is through message boards. Message boards can be great tools for genealogists who are trying to connect with others who have similar interests. When many people participate in these boards, the amount of information that can be shared is tremendous. Message boards are also very convenient and researchers are able to search previous posts to the boards and ask questions to other interested readers around the world 24 hours a day, 7 days a week, 365 days a year.

Genforum.com

Genforum is one of the popular message boards. It requires the researcher to select one of their forums – a surname, country, US state or US county. Below is a screen print of Genforum's home page that shows multiple selections available to the researcher. On the left you can select a letter to go to a surname forum or a country or a US state. You can also type the name of a forum in the text box in the upper right corner and go to a specific forum that you already know the title.

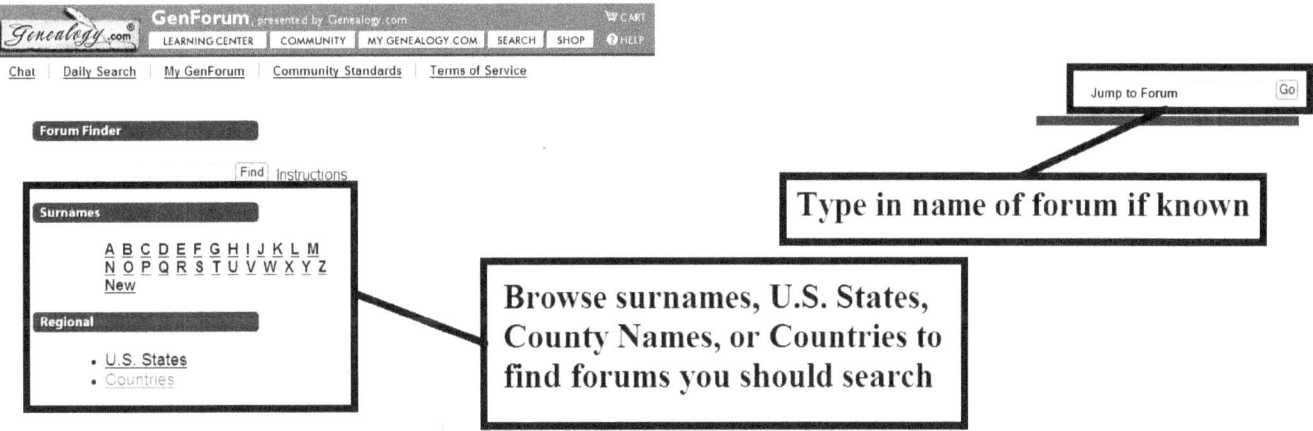

Search Genforum for information

Once you have selected a forum, you can type a key word in the "Search this Forum" text box to narrow the number of posts to review. Next review the headings to select the posts to open and read.

If you need to post a question to this forum, click "Post New Message". You will need to be a registered user and sign in to post this new message or answer a previous post.

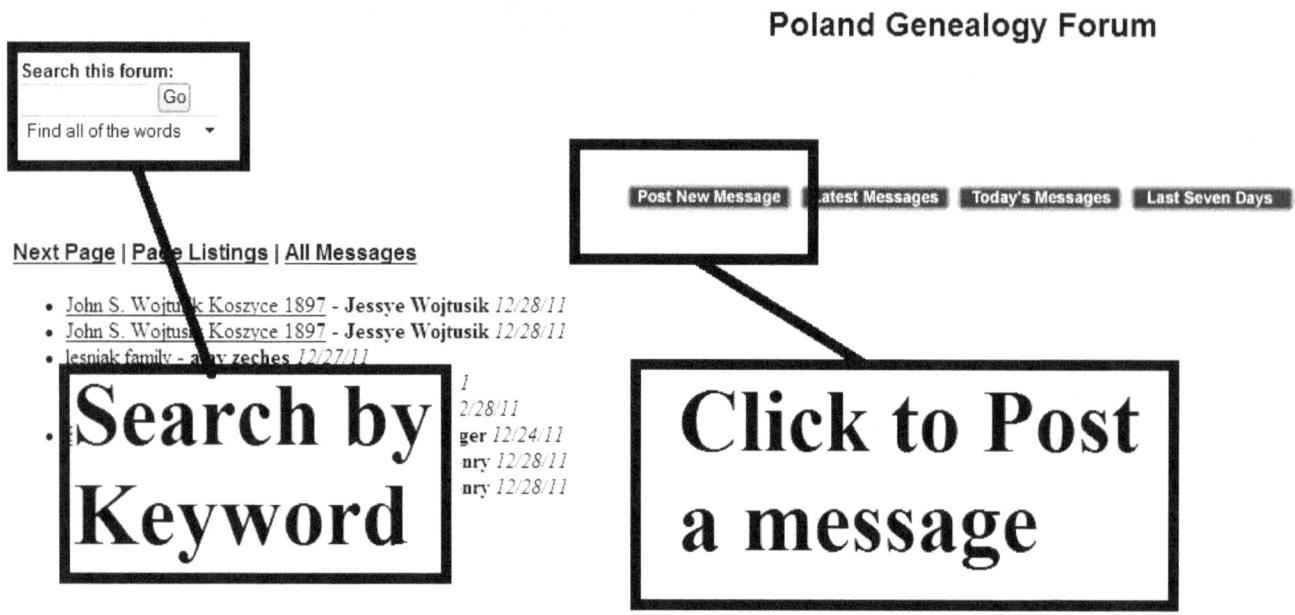

Below is an earlier post that has been opened and below the message is numerous posts of the thread of replies.

Home: Regional: Countries: Hungary Genealogy Forum

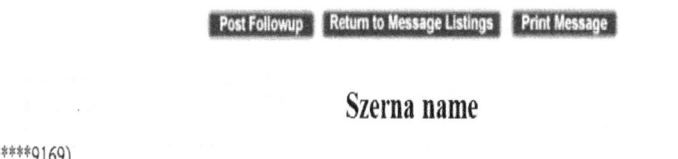

Szerna name

Posted by: Stephen Szabados (ID *****9169)   **Date:** March 29, 2009 at 18:30:14

17740   of 19571 Go

My great-grandmother's maiden name is listed as Szerna on her death certificate and my grandfather's marriage license application. However, I have not found any Hungarian records with that spelling.

Is "Szerna" an "Americanized" version of another Hungarian name?

Notify Administrator about this message?

Followups:

- Re: Szerna name **JosephLaszloKupan** *4/02/09*
  - Re: Szerna name **Stephen Szabados** *4/02/09*
    - Re: Szerna name **JosephLaszloKupan** *4/02/09*
      - Re: Szerna name **Stephen Szabados** *4/02/09*
        - Re: Szerna name **JosephLaszloKupan** *4/02/09*
          - Re: Szerna name **Stephen Szabados** *4/02/09*

Below is the text of a reply to one of my other posts on Genforum that was finally answered after about nine months of waiting.

Heading: *Chmielewski, Zaluski, Zuchowski, Dmochowski, Dmochy, Czyzew, Andrzejewo*
Date: *Sunday, August 17, 2008 4:59 PM*

From: *"xxxxxxx xxxxxxxxx" <xxxxxxx@yahoo.co.uk>*

View contact details
To: xxxxxxxxxxxx@sbcglobal.net

Hi:-) I accidently found your post :

My grandparents were born in Andrzejewo and Dmochy Kudly near Czyzew and south of Lomza. I would like to exchange information with anyone that has ancestors from this area and have the surnames of Chmielewski, Zuchowski, Zaluski and Dmochowski.

My both parents are from Dmochy My dad was born in Dmochy Wochy (Zawistowski) and my mum in Dmochy Kudly(Malinowska but her mother's maiden name Dmochowska) .I am living in UK but my parents are living in Poland in Czyzew and I got my Godfather living in Dmochy so I can ask them some questions if you want

Kindly Regards
Pawel

After numerous exchanges of emails and information it was determined that I was probably related to Pawel's mother. Also Pawel's mother visited the village and borrowed a number of pictures from descendants of my grandfather's brother and below is a picture of my great-grandfather Leopold Zuchowski that Pawel sent to me. This is a great treasure for a little effort.

Leopold Zuchowski – my Great-grandfather

Rootsweb.com

Rootsweb is another website that offers a popular message board. Below is a screen print of the Rootsweb homepage with the Message Board selection option highlighted. The next page shown below is the "Message Board" page and the text box that you will use to search all of the Rootsweb messages. You can also select specific boards to search.

Rootsweb.com Home Page

Rootsweb Message Board

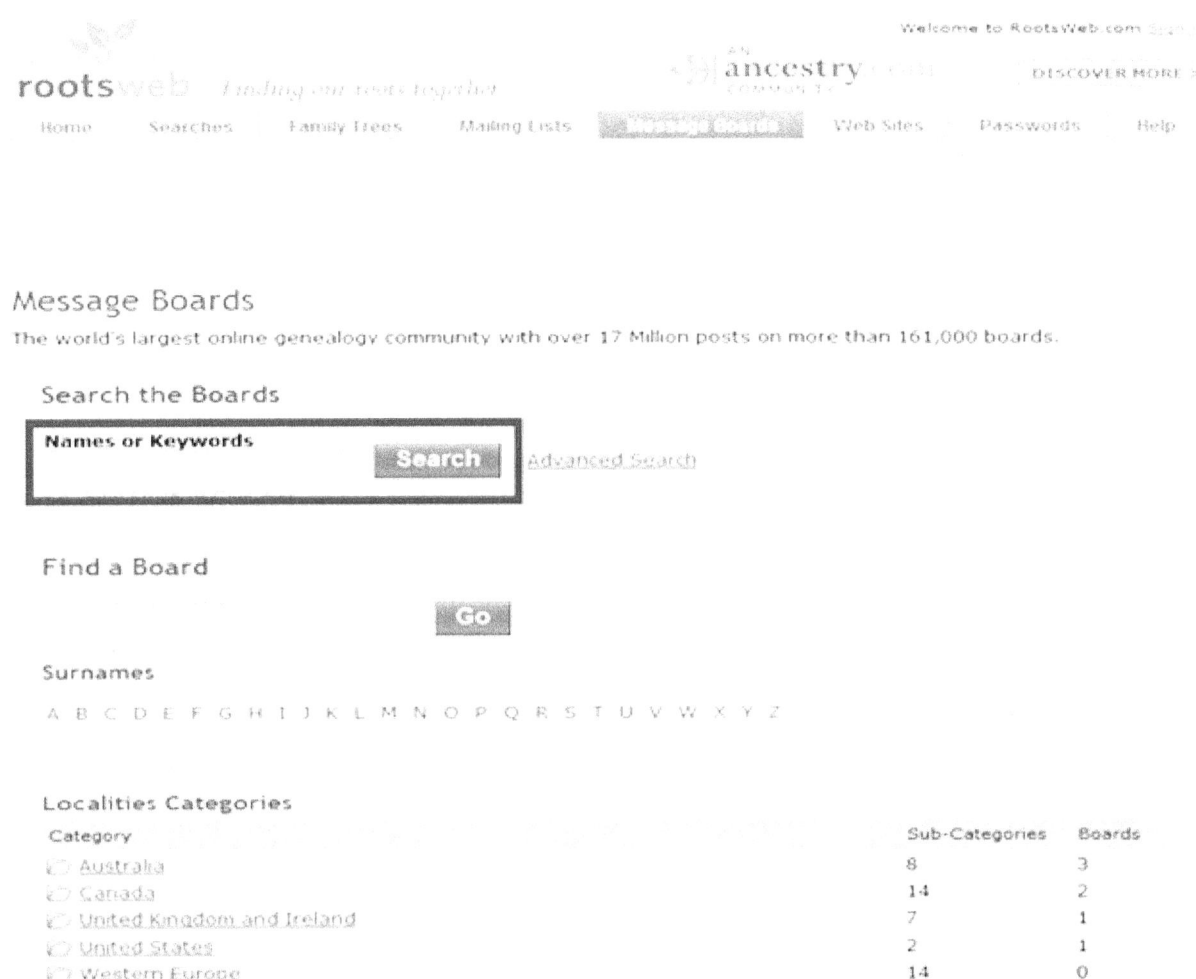

Below is a Sample of results for a search for the surname Dmochowski which is highlighted automatically by Rootsweb software.

Re: Maiden Name of Helen Pietruszka

   Surnames > Pietruszka

Do you know if Rose Dmochowski was married to Alexander?

Re: Maiden Name of Helen Pietruszka

   Surnames > Pietruszka

Yes, Rose's husband was Alex Dmochowski, they lived in Camden, NJ. Annie her sister, my grandmother married Alexander (

Re: Maiden Name of Helen Pietruszka

   Surnames > Pietruszka

My grandfather was the cousin of Alex Dmochowski and I think he and my grandmother met in Camden when my grandfathe

Guidelines and tips to follow when using Message Boards:
1. Only post information on a message board that you are comfortable with being made public. Read your post carefully before you click the send or post button.
2. Read the user agreement for the message board and follow their guideline carefully.
3. Include as much information as possible that pertains to your question or response to avoid confusion. More details should produce responses that are more appropriate to the question.
4. Please type using correct spelling and correct grammar – again to avoid confusion.
5. Be considerate and polite to others at all times.
6. Be concise and try not to ramble.

Use Online Family Trees for Clues

Many websites allow researchers to post the family trees online. Researchers may begin their research using one of these online family trees to chart their family. Some may start with an online tree and then convert to using lineage software on their computer. Some may use only an online tree and some may use both. Whatever the reasons are for the presence of an online family tree finding one or more that will give you a chance to make contact with people searching for the same ancestors. This also gives you a great opportunity to exchange information with these contacts. However, please remember that this information may be very exciting to find but you must do the work and verify its accuracy.

1. The value of searching online family trees would be to provide clues on where to look for the next level in your family tree.
2. The value of maintaining your family tree online is to make contacts with researchers to exchange information.

Below is a sample of the Ancestry.com page that allows a subscriber to search Ancestry's database of family trees. Most other family tree websites offer similar options.

Below is the Ancestry.com page for my grandfather's information. If you have an online family tree only for an online presence, you can post as much or as few details as you desire. It is recommended that you post some details to attract responses from other researchers. The amount of details that I posted for my grandfather may be more extensive than is needed to attract a researcher but I added more information to exchange information with close relatives that I had already contacted and allowed them to visit the family tree without being a subscriber.

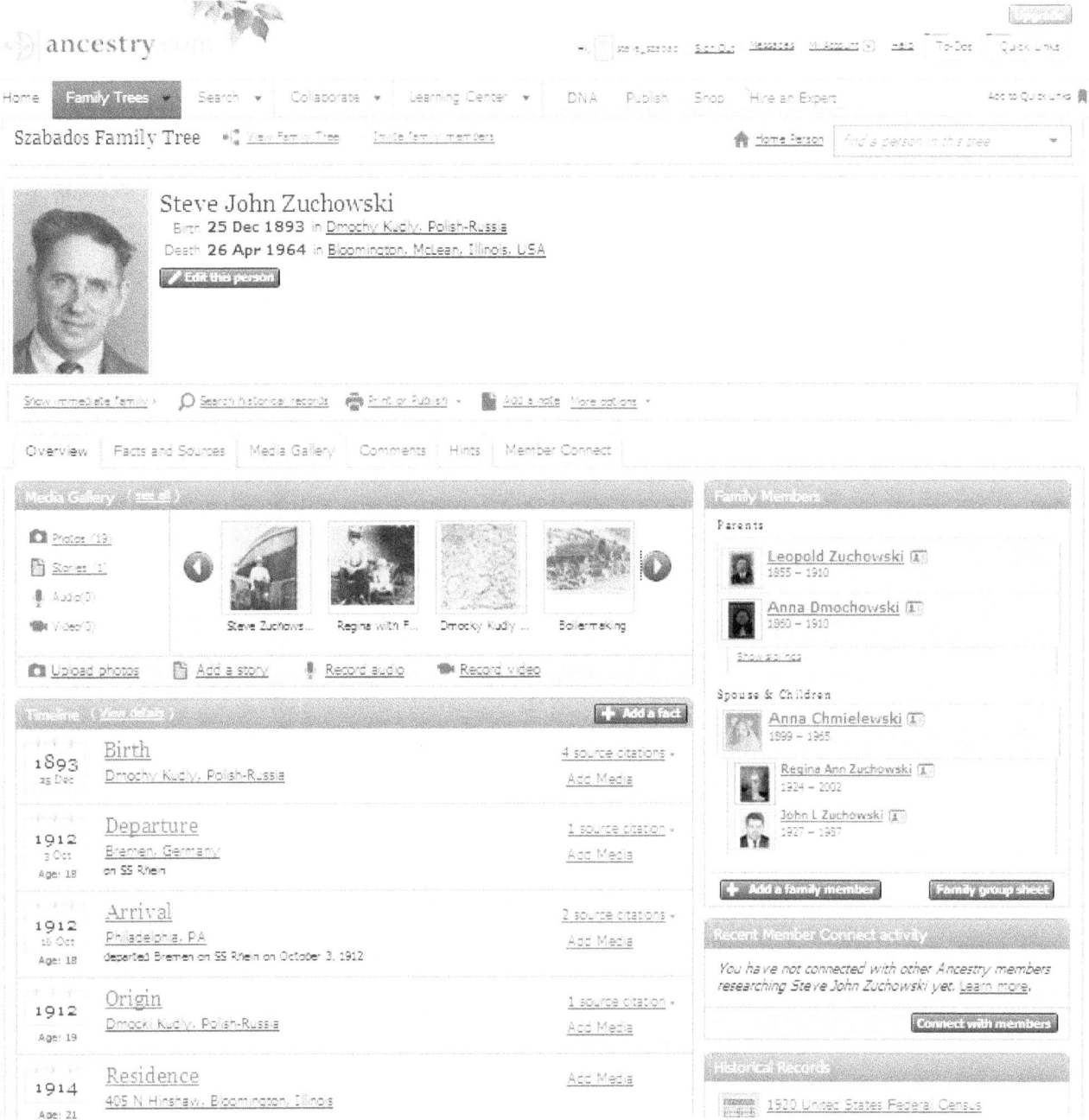

Contact from someone seeing one of my family trees on Ancestry.com

Below is an email that I received from a woman in Germany who turned out to be my daughter-in-law's third cousin and had just started her research. I shared my US research with her and she sent me a small list of German ancestors plus a picture of the house that my daughter-in-law's ancestor sold to bring his family to America. The picture of the house follows the email.

Here is the Email from Kathrin in Germany about my daughter-in-law's family tree:

Itch have Hire Profile auf Ancestry - refunded, in deem waiter Informational angefordert werden
Sunday, July 13, 2008 12:45 PM

From: Kathrin
To: "steve_szabados" <antiquebookworm@sbcglobal.net>

Hi, I`m from Germany, doing research in my ancestry...I`m a grandchild of a born "Volk" from Wahles, Thuringia.

Are you related to John and Terry XXXXXX???

Greets from Germany! Kathrin

House that ancestor of daughter-in-law sold to immigrate to Illinois (picture supplied by Kathrin)

Concerns when posting your family tree on the internet:
- Upload your tree to Ancestry.com – this may get you questions from other people who are researching the same people as you are.
- Be careful to avoid posting information that is private or that you do not want known outside of the family – such as birth, Social Security Number, etc
- Be as accurate as possible. Try to post only confirmed facts to our online tree.

12 CONTINUE YOUR EDUCATION

This book should be used as a starting point in your search for your family history. You should use additional sources to learn more about each topic. These can be books on a specific topic, genealogy programs and conferences, networking with other genealogy researchers, online educational offerings and magazine articles that you find at the library or online. Use these resources to learn more about genealogy research methods and sources..

Below are more details about the above suggestions.

Books

There are many genealogy books available that cover specific topics that can help you find more documents and information about your ancestors. The list below is some of the more popular books, but do not limit your reading to this list.

- **The Organized Family Historian** by Ann Carter Fleming
- **Your Guide to the Federal Census** by Kathleen W. Hinckley
- **Finding Answers in U.S. Census Records** by Loretto Dennis Szucs
- **They Became Americans: Finding Naturalization Records and Ethnic Origins** by Loretto Dennis Szucs
- **American Naturalization Records 1790-1990: What They Are and How to Use Them** by John J. Newman
- **Guide to Finding Your Ellis Island Ancestors** by Sharon DeBartolo Carmack
- **They Came in Ships: A Guide to Finding Your Immigrant Ancestors** Arrival Records by John P. Colletta
- **Guide to Naturalization Records of the United** States by Christina Schaefer
- **Your Guide to Cemetery Research** by Sharon DeBartolo Carmack
- **Organizing Your Family History Search** by Sharon DeBartolo Carmack
- **Unpuzzling Your Past** by Emily Anne Croom

Genealogy Societies

Join a genealogy society and get involved. The society will help you expand your genealogical skills. You will be able to meet fellow genealogists and learn more about research methods from conversations with them. Most societies schedule regular programs and conferences that increase genealogy skills of their members. Another opportunity to learn will come from working on service projects, society committees and at conferences. Besides your learning experiences, it should be fun and rewarding.

Presentations and Conferences

Attending genealogy presentations and conferences in your area is another opportunity to increase your genealogy skills. The programs can be put on by your own society or be put on by nearby societies. Some libraries also schedule genealogy programs regularly. Visit the websites of the genealogy societies in your area and the websites for nearby libraries to see what genealogy programs they have scheduled and then plan to attend.

Online Study

There are many resources available online that can also help improve your genealogy skills.

- The National Genealogical Society offers a home study course that covers the basics of genealogical research.
- Ancestry.com offers many resources on their website. They have archived many articles that have been written by their staff and they also have many videos of the webinars that they have produced over the years. These all can be accessed on their website without being a subscriber.
- Familysearch.org has a collection of videos and articles that are very helpful and can be accessed on their website. You can access their learning tools from their home page by selecting "Learn" on the top toolbar. In their learning section you will then be able to choose to go to their "Wiki" page and search for articles on the topic that you seek. If you select "Resource Courses," you will then be able to choose from a number of videos that are very instructive.

Blogs and Magazines

Reading genealogy blogs and magazines are a way to keep current on what is new in genealogy research.

Blogs

Blogs are online journals that consist of "posts" on various topics. They are usually the work of one person but sometimes are the product of a small group. Most are free but occasionally the authors charge a small subscription fee. Below is a list of blogs that I have found useful:

- **Olive Tree Genealogy** Blog (olivetreegenealogy.blogspot.com) - This blog is the product of one person Lorine McGinnis Schulze and is associated with her website The Olive Tree Genealogy (www.olivetreegenealogy.com). Both the posts on her blog and the information on her website have proved to be very helpful.

- **Dear MYRTLE** (blog.dearmyrtle.com) - Pat Richley-Erickson has been writing genealogy article since 1995 (first in print newspapers and now online). I have found her posts extremely helpful and to the point.

- **Dick Eastman's Genealogy Newsletter** (blog.eogn.com/eastmans_online_genealogy) - Dick Eastman's excellent newsletter is a leading source for genealogy material. The website contains both free content and subscription material.

- **Ancestry Insider** (ancestryinsider.blogspot.com) - The description of this blog found in its masthead is very accurate - *The unofficial, unauthorized view of Ancestry.com and FamilySearch.org. The Ancestry Insider reports on, defends, and constructively criticizes these two websites and associated topics. The author attempts to fairly and evenly support both.*

- **Geneanet Genealogy Blog** (genealogyblog.geneanet.org) - Geneanet is a website (Geneanet.org) that offers help to individual researchers through a free online familytree uploads, forums, document sharing and also publishes a blog.

- **Genealogy Insider Blog** (blog.familytreemagazine.com/insider) - This blog is published by Diane Haddad and the staff of Family Tree Magazine. It has great detailed articles and it well worth the time to visit regularly.

- **Genealogy Roots Blog** (http://genrootsblog.blogspot.com/) – Officially classified as a genealogy magazine, this site is more a blog that provides links to US web sites for vital records, obituaries, etc.

Many genealogy blogs discuss recent develops in genealogy. Try a few and connect regularly via RSS Feeds with the ones that you find useful.

Magazines

Print versions of genealogy magazines are becoming obsolete. Many have stop publication or have gone to online versions. The few that are left have gone to bi-monthly and quarterly publication intervals when they used to be monthly or bi-monthly. Try reviewing some of the issues at your local library before subscribing. If your local library does not have the magazine you are interested in try a larger nearby library.

Below is the list of genealogy magazines that are popular:

- **Genealogy In Time™ Magazine** (http://www.genealogyintime.com/index.html) – a very popular genealogy website. Everything is free. It has powerful search engines, listings of the latest genealogy records, in-depth articles and fun tools to track the latest genealogy blog postings, tweets and genealogy news from around the world.

- **Family Tree Magazine** (http://www.familytreemagazine.com/) – Publishes 7 issues per year in print and online versions. Their website has some free content, although the emphasis is on getting people to subscribe to the print edition of the magazine.

- **Family Chronicle Magazine (**http://www.familychronicle.com/**)** – This is an online version of a print magazine with the same name. There is some free content, with an emphasis on getting people to subscribe to the print edition of the magazine.

- **Internet Genealogy** (http://internet-genealogy.com/) - Offers both online and print versions.

- **Genealogy Magazine** (http://www.genealogymagazine.com/) – This site is more a genealogy store than a magazine. It sells books, databases and articles for tracing your ancestors.

- **The Global Gazette** (http://globalgenealogy.com/globalgazette/index.htm) – This is a genealogy store with some free content.

Social Media

Facebook and Twitter are two exciting communication tools that are having an impact on genealogy research today and are being used by more researchers each day. If you are comfortable using smart phones and tablets, you may want to explore using social media sites to enhance your genealogy research methods. I have not used these resources myself but the following are comments based on information from friends.

- **Facebook** allows the formation of groups that can focus on specific interests. Groups that can help your genealogy research include interests based on ethnicity, surname and locale. Because members of the group have very specific interests, asking a question may get a quick and knowledgeable answer. You can also use groups to interact with your family where you can discuss both social events and family genealogical questions. However, you can not search for the content of old posts and you must scroll down to see them. The success of a Facebook group as a genealogy source is dependant of the number of active participants on any given day and how many are knowledgeable.

- **Twitter** is an online social networking service that enables its users to send and read text-based posts of up to 140 characters, known as "tweets". It can be used to instantly connect to what's most important to you. Follow your friends, experts, favorite celebrities, and breaking news. Twitter can be used to ask a question or your tweets can spread information. You will receive information on your Smartphone, tablet or computer shortly after the question or information is posted to twitter - you do not need to visit a website to see the post. A friend mentioned that they can ask a question and usually have an accurate answer in 15-30 minutes.

People new to genealogy can find help easily on Facebook and Twitter because many genealogy professionals advertise their services on these services. Many researchers post the results of their work on their blogs by tweeting out their URL or by posting it on Facebook.

Summary
Be sure to use all of the sources mentioned above to enhance your genealogical skills. Some are based on traditional methods and some are based on new technologies such as blogs and social media. Each has their strengths and weaknesses but all can be very useful.

As genealogy continues to grow, one or more of these sources may give you a new path to treasures about your ancestors.

CLOSING COMMENTS

Researching your family history can have some very exciting moments. Find your first census record and feel the thrill of seeing a snapshot of your family. I became addicted to genealogy research after finding my grandfather's passenger manifest and had difficulty waiting to see my ancestors in the next document. You can also feel this thrill once you find your first document. Filling in more generations of your family tree and finding more family facts will start to haunt your waking thoughts. Get started and be prepared to make researching your family history a lifelong journey. Just like a great novel, it will be hard to put down.

Try to have a goal in your research. My goals were to learn more about my family's heritage and to preserve what I find for my children and grandchildren. Your goals can be similar to mine or as simple as doing an in-depth study of one of your famous ancestors. Remember that genealogy starts at home. Collect documents, pictures and letters that you and your immediate family have stored away in old shoe boxes in the closet or stuffed in desk drawers. Remember also that it is critical to interview your older relatives to save their memories and oral history.

Be organized in your research. Use genealogy charts and computer software to save the facts that you find on the documents that you find. Organizing your genealogy research will save you time but will also point the way for more research. Use summaries to organize your facts and as a reference tool while doing your research. The information on your summaries can make your research more efficient and help you find more documents and facts. Summaries are also a great way to share your research with your family. Sharing will bring more opportunities for other family members to contribute. Your work may help them remember more oral history and point to more areas to research.

Remember to copy and preserve the documents, letters and pictures that you find. Making electronic copies is a great method of sharing them with your family. Save all originals in a safe place and only travel with copies. Also remember to identify and label the family pictures. Asking relatives to identify who is in the pictures will help extend your family tree and also turn on the memories of the relatives who are helping.

Records you find may be confusing, misleading and wrong. You will need to continually analyze and interpret your information and note where you got your information. As a beginner to genealogy, start now to carefully note where you get every piece of information. Record your information as you find your facts. You may hear arguments that keeping up with sources are time consuming and too much trouble. It isn't fun but without your source information you can't evaluate what you have found. You can't analyze and draw conclusions. And you can't pass along your information because at least one family member will ask, "But how do you know?"

More and more genealogy records are being listed in online databases and these are great sources to begin your research. However there are many more genealogy records stored in libraries and historical archives that also may include your ancestors. Be sure to use all sources in your research and you should be rewarded for your efforts.

Remember that this book should be used as a starting point in your search for your family history. Use books, genealogy programs, genealogy conferences, genealogy societies, online educational offerings and magazine articles to further your genealogy skills. Again once you start your journey it will probably be a lifelong passion.

My last thought that may help you develop the same passion for genealogy as I have is to

"Have fun."

Bibliography

- Allen, Desmond Walls - First Steps in Genealogy, Betterway Books, Cincinnati, Ohio 1998
- Bockman, Jeffrey A. - Give Your Family a Gift That Money Can't Buy, Alenjes publishing, Naperville, Illinois 2007
- Carmack, Sharon DeBartolo - Organizing Your Family History Search, Betterway Books, Cincinnati, Ohio 1999
- Carmack, Sharon DeBartolo - Your Guide to Cemetery Research, Betterway Books, Cincinnati, Ohio 2002
- Carmack, Sharon DeBartolo - You Can Write Your Family History, Betterway Books, Cincinnati, Ohio 2003
- Carmack, Sharon DeBartolo - Guide to Finding Your Ellis Island Ancestors, Betterway Books, Cincinnati, Ohio 2005
- Colletta, John P. - They came in Ships: A Guide to Finding Your Immigrant Ancestors Arrival Records, Ancestry, Salt Lake City, 1993
- Croom, Emily Anne - Unpuzzling Your Past, Betterway Books, Cincinnati, Ohio 2001
- Croom, Emily Anne - The Sleuth Book for Genealogists, Betterway Books, Cincinnati, Ohio 2000
- Croom, Emily Anne - The Genealogist's Companion & Sourcebook, Betterway Books, Cincinnati, Ohio 2003
- Fleming, Ann Carter - The Organized Family Historian, Rutledge Hill Press, Nashville, Tennessee 2004
- Hinckley , Kathleen W. - Your Guide to the Federal Census, Betterway Books, Cincinnati, Ohio 1998
- Kempthorne, Charley - For All Time, a Complete Guide to Writing Your Family History, Boynton/Cook Publishers, Portsmouth, New Hampshire 1996
- Mills, Elizabeth Shown - Evidence Explained : Citing History Sources From Artifacts To Cyberspace, Genealogical Publishing Company, Baltimore, Maryland, 2009
- Mills, Elizabeth Shown - QuickSheet Citing Online Historical Resources, Genealogical Publishing, Baltimore, Maryland 2007
- Newman, John J. - American Naturalization Records 1790-1990: What They Are and How to Use Them, Heritage Quest, Bountiful, UT, 1998
- Quillen, W. Daniel - Mastering Census and Military Records, Cold Spring Press, 2011
- Quillen, W. Daniel - Secrets of Tracing Your Ancestors, Cold Spring Press, 2010
- Quillen, W. Daniel - Mastering Online Genealogy, Cold Spring Press, 2011
- Schaefer, Christina - Guide to Naturalization Records of the United States, Genealogical Publishing, Baltimore, 1997
- Spaltro, Kathleen - Genealogy and Indexing, Information Today, Medford, New Jersey 2003
- Szucs, Loretto Dennis - Finding Answers in U.S. Census Records, Ancestry Publishing, 2001
- Szucs, Loretto Dennis - They Became Americans: Finding Naturalization Records and Ethnic Origins, Ancestry, Salt Lake City, 1998
- U.S. Department of Justice - Foreign Variations and Diminutives of English Names, 1973

Useful Websites (free access unless $$ shown)
- Cyndi's list - http://www.cyndislist.com/
- Ancestry.com ($$) or Ancestry Library Edition (free at local library) - http://www.ancestry.com/
- Family History Centers - http://www.familysearch.org
- Ellis Island Foundation - http://ellisisland.org/
- Castle Garden - http://www.castlegarden.org/searcher.php
- U.S. National Archives - http://www.archives.gov/
- Search Utilities - http://stevemorse.org
- Message board - http://www.rootsweb.ancestry.com/
- Message board - http://Genforum.com

- Bureau of Land Management - http://www.glorecords.blm.gov/
- Genealogy Trails History Group - http://genealogytrails.com/
- Learn to interview - http://genealogy.about.com/cs/oralhistory/a/interview.htm
- Cemetery records - http://www.findagrave.com/
- Cemetery records - http://www.interment.net/
- Veterans Administration graves locator website - http://gravelocator.cem.va.gov
- Iowa WPA cemetery website - http://iowawpagraves.org/
- Newspaperarchive - http://www.newspaperarchive.com/ ($$)
- NewsBank - http://www.newsbank.com/ (available at many libraries)
- Genealogy Bank - http://www.genealogybank.com/gbnk/ ($$)
- ProQuest - http://www.proquest.com/ (available at many libraries)
- Godfrey Memorial Library - http://www.godfrey.org/ ($$)

ABOUT THE AUTHOR

Steve Szabados is a native of Bloomington, Illinois and now lives in Palatine, Illinois. He received a Bachelor of Science Degree from the University of Illinois in Champaign-Urbana, Illinois and a Masters in Business Administration from Northern Illinois University in DeKalb, Illinois. He is a retired project manager. He has been researching his ancestors for about ten years and has traced ancestors back to 1600s New England and 1730's in Poland, Germany, Bohemia and Slovenia. He has given numerous presentations to genealogical groups and libraries in Illinois, Indiana and Wisconsin. His goal is to share his passion for Family History. He is a member of the Polish Genealogical Society of America, Northwest Suburban Council of Genealogists, Illinois State Genealogical Society and he is also a genealogy volunteer at the Arlington Heights Illinois Library. His first book Finding Grandma's European Ancestors outlines four easy steps for the genealogy researcher to find their European ancestors. Steve also is the genealogy columnist for the Polish American Journal and manages his genealogy blog.

If you would like to ask Steve a question about anything in this book, please contact him at S-szabados@sbcglobal.net. Also visit his blog at steveszabados.com

www.ingramcontent.com/pod-product-compliance
Lightning Source LLC
Chambersburg PA
CBHW081830280526
45789CB00007B/2411